Vietnam

The Logic of Withdrawal

Howard Zinn

Vietnam

The Logic of Withdrawal

Haymarket Books
Chicago, IL

© 1967 by Howard Zinn

First published in 1967 by Beacon Press.
This edition published in 2013 by Haymarket Books.
P.O. Box 180165
Chicago, IL 60618
773-583-7884
info@haymarketbooks.org
www.haymarketbooks.org

ISBN: 978-1-60846-305-3

Trade distribution:
In the U.S. through Consortium Book Sales and Distribution, www.cbsd.com
In the UK, Turnaround Publisher Services, www.turnaround-uk.com
In Canada, Publishers Group Canada, www.pgcbooks.ca
In Australia, Palgrave Macmillan, www.palgravemacmillan.com.au
All other countries, Publishers Group Worldwide, www.pgw.com

Special discounts are available for bulk purchases by organizations
and institutions. Please contact Haymarket Books for more information
at 773-583-7884 or info@haymarketbooks.org.

This book was published with the generous support of
the Wallace Global Fund and Lannan Foundation.

Printed in the United States by union labor.

Library of Congress CIP Data is available.

1 3 5 7 9 10 8 6 4 2

To the People of Vietnam

Contents

I. *A Matter of Perspective*

VIETNAM, it seems to me, has become a theater of the absurd.

1. By late 1966, the United States was spending for the Vietnam war at an annual rate of twenty billion dollars, enough to give every family in South Vietnam (whose normal annual income is not more than several hundred dollars) about $5000 for the year. Our *monthly* expenditure for the war exceeds our *annual* expenditure for the Great Society's poverty program.

2. Early in 1966, a new pacification technique was developed by American soldiers. It involved surrounding a village, killing as many young men as could be found, and then taking away the women and children by helicopter. The Americans called this procedure "Operation County Fair."

3. The Pentagon disclosed in 1966 that it had paid to relatives an average of $34 in condolence money for each Vietnamese killed accidentally in American air strikes during that summer. At the same time, according to reports from Saigon, the Air Force was paying $87 for each rubber tree destroyed accidentally by bombs.

4. A *New York Times* dispatch from Saigon, June 21, 1966:

> The United States Air Force turned its attention yesterday to a column of 10 water buffalos sighted along a road just north of the Mugia Pass on the Laotian-North Vietnamese border.
>
> The spokesman said the buffalos were heavily laden with what was suspected to be enemy ammunition. The animals died under fire from F-105 Thunderchief jets. The spokesman said, "There were no secondary explosions."
>
> United States Marine pilots also strafed a column of 11 pack elephants in the mountains 35 miles southwest of Danang in South Vietnam yesterday. Five of the animals were killed

and five others seen to fall. Again there were no secondary explosions.

5. A Chicago newspaper, asked by a reader if it were true that for every enemy soldier it killed in Vietnam the United States was killing six civilians, replied that this was not true; we were killing only *four* civilians for every soldier.

6. Covering the Buddhist revolt against the Ky government in early 1966, *Life* magazine showed a photo of a South Vietnamese soldier coming up behind an unarmed, gowned Buddhist monk and clubbing him unconscious. No comment was made by *Life*. The same page showed Buddhist demonstrators burning an American motorcycle. This was called an "ugly" action.

7. At his press conference on March 22, 1966, at a time of expanding warfare and growing casualties in Vietnam, President Johnson said, among other things: "If I get real depressed when I read how everything has gone bad here, I just ask for the letters from Vietnam so I can cheer up."

8. The January 16, 1965 *Milwaukee Journal* reported that a young man who had studied agricultural economics at the University of Minnesota, learning to aid underdeveloped countries improve their yields, was now an Air Force captain and was using his knowledge to point out productive rice fields in Vietnam, so that United States planes could destroy them with bombs and chemicals.

9. In the spring of 1966, a journalist interviewed an Air Force general in Saigon:

> Journalist: Let me ask you a philosophical question. What is your reply to those who say we ought to stop our bombing —both North and South—and that would bring us closer to negotiating an end to this war?
> General: Well, we were sent out here to do a job, and we're doing it, and we'll stay here until it's done.
> Journalist: Thank you.

10. In March 1966, President Johnson, talking about Vietnam with Columbia University historian Henry Graff, said "proudly"

(as Graff reported it): "I want to leave the footprints of America there."

Isolated oddities can, on investigation, prove to be deviations from an otherwise healthy set of circumstances. Or they may turn out to be small symptoms of a more generalized malady. In such a case, investigation may disclose larger absurdities:

1. The most powerful nation in the world, producing 60 percent of the world's wealth, using the most advanced weapons known to military science short of atomic bombs, has been unable to defeat an army of peasants, at first armed with homemade and captured weapons, then with modern firearms supplied from outside, but still without an air force, navy, or heavy artillery.

2. Declaring its intent to preserve freedom, the United States has supported a succession of military dictatorships in South Vietnam.

3. Again and again President Johnson has insisted that American forces are in Vietnam to repel "aggression" and that "if they'll go home tomorrow, we'll go home." Our actions in South Vietnam have been conducted against a force of which 80 percent to 90 percent are already home (that is, in South Vietnam, where they are from) with the rest from North Vietnam, which is not very far from home. Indeed, if the Geneva Accords are to be taken as a basis (as the United States itself agrees), it is all one country, and *all* our opponents are home. The main fighting against these Vietnamese is conducted now by 350,000 Americans, all of whom are quite far from home, plus 40,000 Koreans, who also are definitely not home. In bombing North Vietnam, our fliers, who are not home, are killing people who are.

4. Government officials have declared that we are at war in Vietnam to stop Chinese "expansion." Available evidence is that there are no Chinese troops in Vietnam, nor anywhere else outside of China. China is, indeed, half encircled by American military bases in Korea, Japan, the Philippines, Formosa, Okinawa, and Thailand—with about 250,000 United States soldiers, sailors, and airmen at those bases.

5. The United States maintains it must continue fighting in

Vietnam so as not to lose prestige among its allies. As the war has continued, the prestige of the United States in Japan (its most important ally in Asia) and in England, France, and West Germany (its most important allies in Europe) has seriously declined.

"Absurdity" is in the mind of the viewer; it involves a simple mental operation. We come across what in itself seems an ordinary fact. But when we place it alongside another fact, we find an incongruity. That other fact may come out of the common pile which most people share or it may come out of the viewer's own life experience. Thus to see a situation as absurd does not depend on the number of facts we know about a situation, but on the way we relate the facts we know—on what we pull out of our memories when a fact presents itself.

Likewise, making moral judgments—as on the war in Vietnam—does not depend mainly on the volume of our knowledge. We find, indeed, that the experts in each field disagree sharply on the most fundamental questions. This is because ethical decisions depend on the relationships in which we place the facts we know.

Therefore what we bring to the common body of evidence in Vietnam—the *perspective* we have—is crucial. It determines what we choose to see or not to see. It determines how we relate the things we see. This perspective varies from one person to another. I think we get closer to wisdom, and also to democracy, when we add the perspectives of other people to our own.

What I want to do in this book is to focus my vision, coming from my own set of experiences, on the data of public record: government documents, newspaper reports, the published work of scholars. To begin, then, I should say a little about the biases that affect my view of the war in Vietnam.

In the midst of World War II, I enlisted in the United States Air Force and flew as a bombardier in the European theater of operations. From beginning to end, I believed fervently that Hitler's force had to be met with force. But when I was packing and labeling my folder of war maps and mementos to go home, I impulsively marked it "Never Again." I had participated in at least one atrocity, and I came away from the war with several conclusions:

(1) that innocent and well-meaning people—of whom I considered myself one—are capable of the most brutal acts and the most self-righteous excuses, whether they be Germans, Japanese, Russians, or Americans;

(2) that one of the guiding rules for an Air Force in possession of large quantities of bombs is: "Get rid of them—anywhere";

(3) that the claims of statesmen and military men to be bombing only "military targets" should not be taken seriously;

(4) that war is a monstrously wasteful way of achieving a social objective, always involving indiscriminate mass slaughter unconnected with that objective; that even World War II, with its stark moral issues—the "best" of all wars—presented agonizing moral questions; and that any situation where right and wrong were *not* so clear, and where human life was being sacrificed, should be regarded with deep suspicion.

Later I was trained as a historian and learned that our country is *capable* of moral absurdities. There was the Spanish-American War, described by an American diplomat as a "splendid little war," though it reeked of corpses on Cuban hillsides and rotten meat fed to soldiers—thousands of whom died of food poisoning.

There were our warships cannonading Vera Cruz in 1914, with hundreds of Mexican civilians killed, because the Mexicans refused to give a 21-gun salute to the American flag.

There was Haiti in 1915, where United States Marines brought "order" by shooting 2000 Haitians, with an Admiral wiring the Secretary of the Navy: "Next Thursday . . . I will permit Congress to elect a President."

There was President McKinley's decision to "civilize" the Filipinos, and Andrew Carnegie's subsequent message to a friend who defended our crushing of the Filipino rebellion: "It is a matter of congratulation that you seem to have about finished your work of civilizing the Filipinos. It is thought that about 8000 of them have been completely civilized and sent to Heaven."

My conclusion was not that the United States was more evil

than other nations, only that she was *just* as evil (although she sometimes had more finesse). It does not take too much study of modern history to conclude that nations as a lot tend to be vicious.

My work in American history led to another idea: that there is no necessary relationship between liberalism in domestic policy and humaneness in foreign policy. Some of our most grotesquely immoral deeds have been committed by "liberals." Take Andrew Jackson's murderous attitude toward the Indians (whom we treated, ironically, as a foreign nation) in the bloody Trail of Tears, or Progressive Theodore Roosevelt's bullying activities in the Caribbean. Take Woodrow Wilson's behavior towards Haiti and Mexico and his carrying the nation, for reasons still inexplicable, into the pointless savagery of the First World War.

During a year off from teaching, I did research on modern Chinese history as a Fellow at the Harvard Center for East Asian Studies. I soon became aware of a great gap between the findings of scholars and the policy of the United States. Official policy seemed to be derived more from lurid headlines in the press than from the balanced findings of the academicians. It was not that the reports of "thought control" in China were wrong; it was that so much else that China had accomplished was ignored. It was not that the Chinese were not aggressive in their statements about the United States; it was that their foreign policy was quite restrained for a proud nation with a new regime. It was not that there was not much that was wrong in Communist China; it was that American policy-makers acted as if there was not much that was wrong with the United States.

This last point was important; the moral failures of other nations had to be seen not in isolation, but against our own failures. It was in this connection that another part of my life influenced my perspective on the problem of Vietnam: my years of living and teaching in a Negro community in the deep South and my involvement in some of the civil rights struggles of the early 1960s. That experience has given me a glimpse of American foreign policy from a special standpoint, one which I will try to explain in the third chapter of this book.

There is one final influence on my thinking which I should mention: the perspective of geographical distance, beginning to see American policy as people in a far-off country saw it. There are many Americans in recent years—Peace Corpsmen, travelers, students—who have been startled by a sudden awareness of how other people see us. My own recent experience was with Japan, and I want to discuss this in the next chapter.

On the basis of these angles of vision, brought to bear on the historical record of the Vietnam war, I am going to argue in the following pages that the United States should withdraw its military forces from Vietnam.

Thus far almost all of the nationally known critics of our Vietnam policy—perceptive as they are—have been reluctant to call for the withdrawal of the United States from Vietnam. Sometimes this is for substantive reasons, which I will discuss later on. But often, I believe, it is because these critics consider total military withdrawal, while logical and right, "too extreme" as a tactical position, and therefore unpalatable to the public and unlikely to be adopted as national policy.

Scholars, who pride themselves on speaking their minds, often engage in a form of self-censorship which is called "realism." To be "realistic" in dealing with a problem is to work only among the alternatives which the most powerful in society put forth. It is as if we are all confined to *a, b, c,* or *d* in a multiple-choice test, when we know there is another possible answer. American society, although it has more freedom of expression, than most societies in the world, thus sets limits beyond which respectable people are not supposed to think or speak. So far, too much of the debate on Vietnam has observed these limits.

To me this is a surrender of the role of the citizen in a democracy. The citizen's job, I believe, is to declare firmly what he thinks is right. To compromise with politicians from the very start is to end with a compromise of a compromise. This weakens the moral force of a citizenry which has little enough strength in the shaping of governmental policy. Machiavelli cautioned the Prince not to adopt the ethics of the Citizen. It is appropriate now to suggest to the Citizen that he cannot, without sacrificing both integrity and power, adopt the ethics of the Prince.

2. *The View from Afar: Japan*

BECAUSE I think perspective is so important, I am going to start as far away from the American environment as possible, looking at the Vietnam war from Japan.

A person who is troubled sometimes consults a friendly outsider for an objective appraisal of his behavior. For United States policy in Vietnam, it seems to me Japan is in many ways an ideal consultant. There is much good will there for Americans; Japan is a capitalist nation; she has democratic liberties roughly comparable to those of the United States; and she is a neighbor of Communist China, which plays such a large part in any analysis of the Vietnam situation.

In June 1966, I was invited to Japan, along with Ralph Featherstone, a field secretary with the Student Nonviolent Coordinating Committee. Our hosts were Japanese intellectuals of varying political beliefs—journalists, novelists, poets, philosophers. We traveled north to south through Japan, from Hokkaido to Hiroshima and Fukuoka, and across the East China Sea to Okinawa. We had long, intense discussions with students and faculty at fourteen universities in nine different cities. We spoke at big meetings and small ones, at tea gatherings and beer sessions, with trade unionists and housewives. We found them virtually unanimous in their belief that United States policy in Vietnam was not just a bit awry, but profoundly wrong.

Again it is a matter of perspective. I once saw an eerie ten-minute motion picture called *The Fisherman*, in which a happy angler hauls sleek, fat, leaping fish out of the ocean and piles them lifeless on the beach, meanwhile devouring candy bars from his lunchbox. He finally runs out of food. Restless, unhappy, he sees a paper sack nearby with a sandwich in it, bites into the sandwich, and is hooked! He digs his feet frantically into the sand, but he is dragged—twisting, struggling at the end of a line—into the sea. The effect on the viewer is a sudden reversal of role, both horrifying and healthful, in which, for the first time, he sees himself, The Fisherman, from the standpoint of the Fish.

Something like that happens when you spend time in Japan, talking to the Japanese about American policy in Vietnam. The brutality of the war we are waging, no matter how sharply we feel it on occasion, has the quality of fiction as it appears on television screens or in news columns. Always at hand to "explain" the bombing of villages, the death toll of civilians, the crushing of Buddhist dissidents, are earnest liberals (Humphrey and Goldberg), "realistic" experts (Rostow), genial spokesmen for the administration (Rusk and McNamara). We listen with the languor of a people who have never been bombed, who have only been the bombardiers. Our occasional protests somehow end up muted and polite.

The Japanese have had a more intimate association with death, both as killers and as victims. We in America still cling to the romance of war that is not really war, but Terry and the Pirates, Defending the Free World, or LBJ in a Green Beret. For the Japanese, the Kamikaze pilots, and then the turnabout—Hiroshima and Nagasaki—wore off all the sheen. Out of this experience, they have wanted desperately to speak to Americans.

Featherstone and I were in Tokyo, at Meiji University. Ken Kaiko, a novelist, was telling about four months he had spent taking notes on the front lines in Vietnam, mostly with American soldiers: "It used to be said in Vietnam that it is disastrous to be born a man—you are drafted and killed; it is better to be a woman. But in South Vietnam today, a woman has a child at each side and one in her belly, and must still flee the American bombs." He had seen it himself, he said, that the Americans could not distinguish Vietcong from the air—no matter what the official assurances were—and they simply killed whomever they could, in the target area.

It was Kaiko who in 1965 helped collect money for a full-page ad in *The New York Times,* a plea to Americans:

> Japanese learned a bitter lesson from fifteen years of fighting on the Chinese mainland: weapons alone are of no avail in winning the minds and allegiance of any people. . . . America's conduct of the war in Vietnam is alienating the sympathy of the Japanese.

This last point was corroborated over a year later by the *Times* correspondent in Tokyo, Robert Trumbull, who wrote (September 28, 1966): "Opinion polls have indicated that most Japanese oppose the United States position in Vietnam, although the Sato Government supports it." A Japanese journalist of long experience with a conservative newspaper said to me: "The polls show 80 percent of the Japanese opposed to United States policy in Vietnam. Emotionally, it is closer to 100 percent."

We saw this again and again as we moved through Japan. In Kyoto, a pediatrician spoke up from the audience. Our interpreter—a poet and former Fulbright scholar in America—explained that the speaker was Dr. Matsuda and that his books on child care have sold in the millions; he is known as the Benjamin Spock of Japan. Dr. Matsuda said: "What the United States does not understand is that Communism is *one* of the ways in which underdeveloped countries can become organized. Its reaction to this phenomenon in the world is neurotic."

Matsuda, a hearty, vigorous man in his fifties, went on: "Perhaps the United States needs . . ." Our interpreter hesitated over the end of the sentence, translating it first as "a laxative" and then correcting himself: ". . . a sedative!"

At that meeting in Kyoto, a mountain-rimmed city of temples, shrines, and pagodas, over a thousand people—students, faculty, townspeople—came to talk about Vietnam. A 92-year-old man, dean of the Buddhist priests in this holy city, spoke: "The American concept of freedom violates the principle of self-determination. It is the kind of liberalism that expresses only the purpose of the American state." And a Zen Buddhist priest, head shaven, in black robes and white scarf, said: "There is a major law in Buddhism: not to kill. Mass killing should not go on; that is the simple slogan that binds Japanese Buddhists with Buddhists in North and South Vietnam. And this message should be brought to America."

I had slept the night before in a 700-year-old Buddhist temple and in the morning was taken to the altar, with its ornate gold carvings, the dishes of fresh fruit before it, the flowers, the prayer cushions, the little percussion instruments alongside the sutras. Leaning against the altar was an enlarged photo of a Buddhist monk in Saigon, sitting in flames.

It was in Kyoto that a young professor of astronomy spoke up from the audience, with great feeling: "As a child, I was machine-gunned by an American plane. And at that moment there came a shock of realization that it was a human being that pulled the trigger. I wanted so much to have been able to say to him: 'Please don't pull the trigger!' It seems that now, once again, we must say this to the machine-gunners of the world. Please—don't pull the trigger!"

We took the night train to Hiroshima, along the inland sea touched by mountains and beautiful in the predawn. We talked with students at Hiroshima University and to survivors of that day when, after one long scream, the city died: a professor whose left eye is missing; a fragile girl who spoke halting English in a voice so soft one had to strain to hear: "I was inside my mother when the bomb came." A professor of politics at Hiroshima University, with thick black hair and horn-rimmed spectacles, came back to Dr. Matsuda's point about Communism. "It is the idea that Communism is the root of *all* trouble in the world which has brought the Vietnam war."

In Japanese universities you find many men who spent time in jail for opposing Japanese aggression in the thirties. At Nagoya, sprawling, smoky—the Detroit of Japan—we were met by Professor Shinmura, who in 1936–37 published a humanist magazine called *Sekai Bunka* (*World Culture*) until he was seized by the police. Quiet, gray-haired, a little stooped, Shinmura is a specialist in French literature, and after release from prison he made a living by anonymously translating the writings of Rolland, Diderot, and others.

He took us to a lounge where others of the faculty were waiting for us: several philosophers, a theoretical physicist, a sociologist, a specialist in Oriental history, a professor of Japanese literature, and one Westerner—a tall, young Frenchman just back from the University of Saigon. I asked: how many members of this faculty support American policy in Vietnam? There were 600 on the faculty, including graduate assistants. No one knew any who supported American policy.

I kept asking this question wherever I went. In Osaka, a professor of international affairs replied that he thought perhaps one person on the whole faculty supported American policy. At a large meeting in Osaka I had publicly asked students who were in favor of the American position to speak up. My interpreter, a young chemistry professor with a doctorate from the University of Minnesota, said: "You can't expect anyone here to take a pro-United States position."

To the Japanese we met, it was so clear that America was in the wrong that they could not understand why anyone could believe President Johnson and his cabinet members. How could the United States be "fighting aggression," they asked, when the "enemy" consisted entirely of Vietnamese, mostly Southerners, and *no* Chinese? The official South Vietnamese army had shown little enthusiasm, and so 300,000 American troops, transported across the Pacific, had taken over the war. "No country should be permitted, as the United States is doing, to smuggle counter-revolution to another country," said a professor of literature at Hosei University in Tokyo.

Two planes, a jolting bus ride, and an auto trip through flooded, fresh-plowed fields, brought us to Sendai in northern Honshu. In rectangles of black mud marked off by willowy grass, women, bent low, their bicycles nearby, were transplanting rice seedlings. The streets were crowded with children in school uniforms, bookbags strapped to their backs, and teen-age girls on bikes wearing fresh aprons. A thousand students had gathered at Tohoku University for four hours of talk, with a long question-and-answer period. When this was over and we returned, tired, to our quarters at the Cooperative, we found fifty students waiting for us in the lobby, eager to continue the discussion. We trooped out in the night to a park, the fellows and girls sat cross-legged on the grass, and we talked into the small hours of the morning. There in the cool darkness of Sendai, I wondered why fifty Japanese kids would stay out after midnight to discuss the war in Vietnam, when Japan was only a minor accessory to American action. At the time the United States was helping the French crush the Algerian revolt, did any group of American students ever gather in the park at midnight to brood over this? Did a thousand ever meet to protest it?

By the end of our trip the answer was becoming clear; it lay in the Japanese people's intense consciousness of their own recent history. Again and again, at virtually every meeting, there arose the accusation: "You are behaving in Asia as we once did." There is widespread and vocal recognition of Japan's own sins, from the Manchurian invasion of 1931 to Pearl Harbor. Japanese scholars have done much research on those years, and they see in American actions in Vietnam many of the same characteristics displayed by Japan in the thirties.

Unlike the Nazis, the Japanese did not abruptly replace parliamentary democracy with authoritarian dictatorship. Rather, there was an almost imperceptible growth of the power of the military within an outwardly parliamentary system. When the Japanese took Manchuria in 1931, then attacked China proper in 1937 and moved into Southeast Asia in 1940, they did not declaim crassly of world conquest as did Hitler, but spoke of a "co-prosperity sphere" which they were creating in Asia for the benefit of all.

I asked Professor Maruyama of Tokyo University, one of Japan's most distinguished scholars, about this analogy. A political scientist and prolific author, who five years ago was invited to Harvard as a visiting professor, Maruyama is in his forties, smokes a pipe, has a sharp, strong nose and a warm smile. "There are many differences," he said, "but one crucial element is quite the same: the apologies and justification created by both governments for what is basically an attempt by a strong nation to create a base of power inside a weaker one. Both Japan and the United States had difficulties and made excuses. The United States blames its difficulties in winning the Vietnamese war on China and North Vietnam. Japan attributed her failures not to the stubborn resistance of the Chinese but to the aid given China by Great Britain and the United States. Japan declared that its aim was to emancipate the people of Southeast Asia and to bring them economic development, just as the United States speaks now about economic and social reform while it carries on an essentially military action in Vietnam."

American commentators have a habit of dismissing Japanese criticism of our foreign policy as the work of Communists or, more vaguely, "leftists." This is comforting until one reflects that most public opinion in the world, even in countries allied to us, is to the left of ours. The United States has become, since that period when Europe's monarchs feared we would spread the doctrine of revolution, a conservative nation. Even our "liberals" are conservative by global standards.

For instance, Maruyama had just met with McGeorge Bundy in Tokyo: "Now Mr. Bundy has a new job as head of the Ford Foundation. But psychologically, he is still with the government. He turned on me in a fury when I told him that never has the prestige of the United States been so low abroad, due to Vietnam."

Our companions and interpreters in Japan were young nonparty intellectuals—two journalists, three novelists, a film producer, a poet, a philosopher—who decided early in 1965 to form a group called *Beheiren* dedicated to ending the Vietnam war. Their chairman, Oda Makoto, is a wry, 34-year-old novelist, big, tousle-haired, with unpressed coat and trousers, who refuses to wear a tie no matter how formal the occasion. Oda is critical of Communist China, but with no more heat than he is critical of Japan or America. He sees it as a new society with the truculence that new regimes generally show, but he does not see it as a threat to the rest of Asia. Like other Japanese intellectuals, Oda believes the United States is reacting to China with hysteria

—and that people in Vietnam are dying unnecessarily because of this.

United States officials keep saying they are acting for the benefit of Asia, but Japan is a prime example of the fact that Asians themselves do not welcome the United States presence. The only countries giving substantial aid to the American military effort (Korea, Thailand) are those which are economically subservient to the United States, under its military occupation, and controlled by elites which can ignore popular will. Veteran correspondent Harrison Salisbury wrote from Asia (July 26, 1966) in *The New York Times*:

> It is not only in the Communist world that opinion is aligned almost entirely against the American Vietnam policy. It is almost impossible to find any substantial public Asian support for it except within those nations benefiting directly from the huge United States investment, such as Thailand.

Asian opinion today seems to agree with what Harvard historian Edwin Reischauer wrote in 1954 in *Wanted: An Asian Policy,* that a policy based largely on stopping Communism is "a dangerous oversimplification of our Asian problem."

There are American troops in Japan (under the much resented Security Treaty of 1960), and part of Japan's territory, Okinawa, has been converted by the United States into one of the most powerful military bases in the world. ("Please tell your fellow Americans," a Tokyo University sociologist said, "that the majority of Japanese do not think these military bases protect Japan's security—in fact, they think these endanger our security.") Nonetheless, the government of Premier Sato, while nodding and bowing to the United States State Department, keeps a wary eye on the Japanese public, knowing popular feeling. A high government official told several of us, off the record, that Japan would like to speak its mind on Vietnam to the United States but does not feel independently strong enough to do so.

Japan is something of an embarrassment to the United States government, because it was under America's postwar tutelage that she put into her new Constitution the statement

". . . never again shall we be visited with the horrors of war through the action of government." Article 9 contains a silent reproach to what the United States is doing in Vietnam: ". . . the Japanese people forever renounce war as a sovereign right of the nation and the threat or use of force as a means of settling international disputes." It is the old human story, the little boy nurtured by his family on the Biblical exhortation Thou Shalt Not Kill, watching his father return, gun still smoking, from a mission of murder.

The Japanese are trying to speak to us, but we will not listen. In a short span of time they have been both Fish and Fisherman. We in the United States have never had to struggle at the end of the hook—and lose. We have no Hiroshima, no city of the blind and maimed, no professors still haggard from long terms in jail. Although on a number of occasions we have been a Fisherman, we have never been forced (as have the Japanese) to recognize our deeds, to bow, to apologize, to promise a life of peace. We have, in other words, never been caught.

Those countries who *have* been caught are now trying to speak to us. Not only Japan, but other friends and allies whose criticism cannot be easily dismissed as "Communist." British public opinion, despite Prime Minister Wilson's cautious approval, has been consistently critical of American policy. Konrad Adenauer, as ardent an anti-Communist as anyone in the American government, said to *New York Times* correspondent C. L. Sulzberger (reported in his column of August 7, 1966): "I would get out of Vietnam. . . . This wouldn't be the first war broken off in the middle. You can't get out by going more strongly in. If I take a road and find myself going in the wrong direction, I see no purpose in continuing along it. I take another road."

The European view was bluntly summarized by George Lichtheim, writing in *Commentary*, July 1966:

> . . . the question (apparently taken seriously by some people in Washington) of why the West Europeans cannot be conscripted into a crusade to help an Oriental cardboard Mussolini in Saigon maintain his comic-opera regime a week or a month longer, has ceased even to be funny. There was a time

when thinking people in London or Paris made an earnest attempt to decipher the mental processes of President Johnson and his advisers. That time is past. No one bothers any more to try to understand why the Americans are behaving as they do: it is accepted that they must, and will, learn from bitter experience, as others have done before them.

What Lichtheim says of European opinion is almost exactly what I found among the Japanese through only a brief, intense, impressionistic survey.

Such are some of the views from a distance. Now I want to take a look at another viewpoint, this one right in our midst— the viewpoint of the Negro American.

3. *A View from Within: The Negro*

THERE IS no one Negro view on Vietnam, any more than there is one white view on Vietnam. But there are such clear signs of hostility to United States policy in Vietnam among important sections of the Negro population that it may be useful for the rest of us to take notice and to inquire: Why?

The signs are unmistakable. They appear quickly, in the press or in personal encounter, then are scattered, gone—and perhaps all I am doing here is pulling some of them together to remind us of what I believe is a significant pattern of opinion.

A Negro field worker for the Student Nonviolent Coordinating Committee told me last year in Mississippi: "You know, I just saw one of those Vietcong guerrillas on TV. He was dark-skinned, ragged, poor, and angry. I swear, he looked just like one of us."

This was an individual reaction, but the Negro organizations have spoken. Of the five major civil rights groups, three (CORE, SNCC, and Dr. Martin Luther King's Southern Christian Leadership Conference) have all declared themselves strongly against U.S. policy in Vietnam, and indeed urged that the United States withdraw.

Never before in the history of this country have Negroes expressed such fierce opposition to the government's foreign policy. And this in spite of the general Negro warmth toward the New Deal, Fair Deal, and Great Society. A columnist for the *Amsterdam News,* the most important newspaper in Harlem and one of the most influential newspapers in the Negro world, wrote on August 21, 1965:

> President Johnson's Great Society is bursting into full bloom. Never has so much been done for so many in so short

a time. . . . But I, for one, have not said a word, and I know at least twenty others . . . men and women, white and colored . . . who have had the same impulse, but have found themselves unable to express words of praise. Because they catch in every throat.

All the accomplishments fade into insignificance. All the progress is shadowed just as all of it can be swiftly undone, by the horror, the spectre, the glaring immorality of Vietnam.

The statements of the more militant civil rights groups (SCLC, CORE, and SNCC) have been even stronger. In January 1966, SNCC said, in its first comment on the war, unanimously approved by its staff of over a hundred field workers:

We believe the United States government has been deceptive in its claim of concern for the freedom of the Vietnamese people, just as the government has been deceptive in claiming concern for the freedom of colored people both in the United States and in other countries. . . . Our work in the South and in the North has taught us that the United States government has never guaranteed the freedom of oppressed United States citizens and is not prepared to end the rule of terror and suppression within its own borders.

Referring to the murder of Samuel Younge, a Negro student in Tuskegee, SNCC said:

Samuel Younge was murdered because United States law is not being enforced. Vietnamese are murdered because the United States is pursuing an aggressive policy in violation of international law. . . .

We maintain that our country's cry of "preserve freedom in the world" is a hypocritical mask behind which it squashes liberation movements which are not bound, and refuse to be bound, by the expediencies of the United States cold war policies. . . .

We are therefore, in sympathy with and support the men in this country who are unwilling to respond to the military draft and thereby contribute their lives to United States aggression in Vietnam.

Stokely Carmichael of SNCC is unsparing in his criticism of Negroes who fight in Vietnam, calling them "black mercenaries."

Several months after this, in April 1966, the Southern Christian Leadership Conference, led by Dr. King, adopted another strong resolution at a time when the Buddhist revolt was being crushed by the Ky government with the complicity of the United States:

> American policy has become imprisoned in the destiny of the military oligarchy. Our men and equipment are revealed to be serving a regime so despised by its own people that, in the midst of conflict, they are seeking its overthrow. Not only the Vietcong but basic institutions of the South Vietnam society, Buddhists, Catholics and students, are expressing contempt for the bankrupt government we have blindly supported and even exalted.
>
> The immorality and tragic absurdity of our position is revealed by the necessity to protect our nationals from the population and army we were told were our cherished allies. . . .
>
> SCLC, as an organization committed to nonviolence, must condemn this war on the grounds that war is not the way to solve social problems. Mass murder can never lead to constructive and creative government or to the creation of a democratic society in Vietnam.

The staff of CORE, which in the summer of 1965 had pressed for and indeed passed a resolution opposing the government's policy in Vietnam, but was pressured by James Farmer to withdraw this, became uninhibited in its criticism of the war when Floyd McKissick became its national chairman. McKissick was one of five Americans who visited Cambodia in the summer of 1966 and found in a frontier village the body of a young pregnant woman, shot to death by a strafing American helicopter the day before. This only confirmed his already bitter feelings about United States behavior in the war.

What of the mass of Negroes outside these organizations? Negro opinion on foreign policy is varied and fluid and shifts rapidly—even within the same person—based on that person's *latest* mood toward the national government. The Negro has had a strong need (like any minority group) to identify himself with the majority, so that often he appears more patriotic than others. But this patriotism is a very thin membrane which, when punctured by some immediate event revealing American racism, releases a fundamental anger at the nation and a distrust of its policies. The turbulence of the struggle at home, coinciding with such a blatantly cruel war as that in Vietnam (whose victims are largely nonwhite), has lacerated again and again the Negro's vulnerable loyalty to America.

As one bit of evidence, I would point to the case of Julian Bond, the SNCC worker elected to the Georgia State Legislature. I would guess that the Negro voters in Julian Bond's Atlanta constituency (a neighborhood in which I and my family lived for seven years), if polled on the Vietnam issue in isolation from other issues, would have reacted along a wide spectrum, from hostility to support, in relation to Lyndon Johnson's policy. But when Bond was expelled by the Georgia Legislature for refusing to repudiate SNCC's criticism of the Vietnam war, local backing for him was so overwhelming that no opponent could be found to run against him in the next election. The *race* mood determines, from moment to moment, the Negro attitude toward Vietnam. In World War II there was such a strong element of anti-racism in the fight against the century's arch-racist, Adolf Hitler, that Negroes could to a large extent be persuaded to support the war. But in the Vietnam war, the situation is different: The foe is not an Anglo-Saxon racist but a mass of poor, dark-skinned peasants who resemble in many aspects of their lives the Negroes of the American rural South.

From time to time incidents in the war, like one reported on American television March 13, 1966, release the pent-up anger of Negroes against a white society that, with an incredibly innocent obliviousness, makes their everyday life miserable. Vietcong rebels had overrun a Special Forces base, occupied by troops of the government of South Vietnam and some American military. United States helicopters flew in to evacuate the Americans, leaving the Vietnamese behind. South Vietnamese rushed the helicopters in their desperation, and the United States soldiers drove them away with gunfire, shooting thirty or forty of them, with undisclosed casualties. It was a complicated scene, but it was hard to avoid the conclusion that by some deeply imbedded principle guiding American conduct, the lives of white Americans were worth more than the lives of Asiatics—even those "on our side."

The charge most often flung at the Johnson administration by Negroes in connection with the Vietnam war can be summed up in one word: hypocrisy. If the government is dedicated to the expansion of freedom in far-off parts of the world, then why is it not equally dedicated to freedom for the Negro at home?

The liberal replies: But it *is*—look at the Civil Rights Acts, the White House Conferences, the speeches by LBJ.

The Negro responds: My real problem is not what it says in the law books, but how much money I have in my pocket. The Negro compares the magnitude of national effort to bring what is claimed to be "freedom" to 13 million people in South Vietnam, with the magnitude of the effort for 15 million Negroes who are poor at home. He compares the $2 billion spent each month on the war with the pitiful sums of money spent on behalf of the Negro. He compares the willingness to commit mass murder in Vietnam, presumably justified by "freedom," with the unwillingness of the federal government to arrest on the spot a sheriff in Mississippi whom FBI men watch beating a Negro. He compares the 350,000 soldiers sent to Vietnam with the frequent refusal of the federal government to send even a handful of marshals to protect Negroes from violence. He compares all the spurious legalistic argument to explain why the federal government cannot protect civil rights workers in the South with the crass violations in Vietnam of international agreements, to say nothing of one of the most important provisions in the United States Constitution, giving Congress alone the power to declare war.

Mississippi Negroes pleaded with the federal government in early June 1964 for protection in what was obviously going to be a dangerous summer. A busload of black Mississippians traveled 1000 miles to present evidence in Washington on the need for such protection, and constitutional lawyers proved that the federal government had all the legal authority it needed to grant this. But the Mississippi Negroes were met with silence, and thirteen days later Schwerner, Goodman, and Chaney, who had to travel unprotected into Neshoba County, were murdered. Even after the murders, when once again asked to supply protection, the federal government gave various arguments: it would violate "the federal system"; not enough marshals were available. But when various tottering regimes in South Vietnam pleaded for help, the government sent thousands of troops across the Pacific.

A brief item from *The New York Times* of June 22, 1966 helps explain the bitterness of Negro militants when the federal government asks support for its massive military effort in Vietnam. It describes a series of acts of violence against Negroes marching into Philadelphia, Mississippi, and goes on to say: "Philadelphia's ten policemen, including two Negroes, and a group of Neshoba County deputy sheriffs watched most of the violence without moving to stop it. At least two Justice Department lawyers and an undetermined number of Federal Bureau of Investigation agents were present as *observers*." (My emphasis.)

Bob Moses, the pioneer of the Mississippi civil rights struggle, summed it up: "Our criticism of Vietnam policy does not come from what we know of Vietnam, but from what we know of America."

The hypocrisy is seen also in United States policy toward those African states where blacks are still controlled by a white minority. If the United States cares enough about "freedom" to make a major military effort in Asia, why has it been so consistently reluctant even to support economic sanctions against the most brutally racist country in the world—South Africa? On June 17, 1965, the Special Committee on Apartheid of the United Nations, calling for "total economic sanctions" against South Africa, according to *The New York Times* of June 18, 1965, "expressed concern that Britain and the United States continued to oppose Security Council action."

Similarly, United States softness toward Portugal's colonialism is contrasted with the hardness in Southeast Asia. On May 2, 1966, professors at the predominantly Negro Lincoln University, in a letter to Senator Fulbright, opposed the nomination of William Tapley Bennett as ambassador to Portugal, pointing out that "in spite of votes by overwhelming majorities within the United Nations General Assembly demanding that Portugal admit the principle of self-determination for its colonies, and despite the persistent refusal of Portugal to act, the United States has consistently voted against United Nations sanctions to induce Portuguese compliance."

Some Negro civil rights workers compare the American fear of revolutionary change in the world to the white South's fear of social change. In this analogy, Lyndon Johnson appears as a kind of global Governor Wallace, sending out the troops to quell demonstrations of the aggrieved and refusing to understand that a group which has suffered over the centuries, once aroused, will not simply retire into the shadows by the threat or use of force. The United States no more understands the psychology of the hungry peasants of the world than the white South has understood the thinking of the Negro. It does not understand the mind of the revolutionist, and this has important implications for the "domino theory." Even a total military victory in Vietnam would not prevent another insurrection from developing the next week in another part of Asia or Latin America, in the presence of deep grievances—just as the beating and killing of Negroes did not stop the marches, the demonstrations, the spread of rebelliousness in the South.

It may offend admirers of the Great Society to hear Lyndon Johnson compared to George Wallace, but consider: to white Alabamans, Wallace has appeared as a kindly, genial statesman, well-meaning and bringing economic progress; they have been mystified by the stubbornness of the Negro revolt and thus have reacted with a violent anger—much as Johnson has reacted in Vietnam.

The analogy can be carried further. The white South, refusing to believe that local Negroes had genuine grievances about which they were disturbed, attributed the demonstrations to "outside agitators." Similarly, the Johnson administration cannot seem to believe that there were genuine grievances in South Vietnam which led to guerrilla warfare, and so it blames the war on "outside infiltration" from North Vietnam, or outside "instigation" from Communist China. There has been infiltration from North Vietnam, and help from Communist China. But so was there "outside" aid to the Southern Negro from Northern Negroes and Northern whites. In neither case, however, does this fact of outside support obliterate a more fundamental truth, that the insurgent energy was indigenous, supplied by severe local problems, and indeed could not have become a major movement unless these problems existed.

The United States government has drawn a kind of curtain around itself to keep out a barrage of criticism from abroad of our Vietnam policies. This is strikingly like the way Alabamans and Mississippians for many years tuned out of the indignation expressed in other parts of the country, listening only to one another, reaffirming their belief that they were right and everyone else in the world wrong.

Both in the American South and in South Vietnam, there is an oversimplification of issues. This is done by the use of symbolic words to arouse emotions and prevent a rational consideration of the complex problems of human relations. In the South, the standard epithet has always been the word "nigger"—which destroys the individuality of the Negro so that the white man can develop an undifferentiated reaction of hatred and contempt for anyone so designated, whatever his unique qualities of character. In American foreign policy, the epithet is "Communist"—which may *begin* to describe a situation in the way the term "nigger" *begins* to describe the person so designated, but which hardly gets to the distinctions that are so crucial in a world where "Communism" has many forms.

Perhaps the crowning hypocrisy is that the national administration, which welcomed with such enthusiasm the adoption of nonviolence by Negroes under direct attack and responded with such alarm when Negroes began only to *speak* about defending themselves, has used such frightful force in a situation where this nation has not been attacked. Even with all the recent emphasis by Negro militants on the right of self-defense, no leader has suggested that Negroes invade the white community with guns and bombs as a *preventive* action to forestall possible attacks on them in the future. Yet this is essentially what the United States is doing in Vietnam.

Toward the end of the tense summer of 1964, many of us who were in Mississippi drove into Neshoba County to attend a memorial service for Schwerner, Chaney, and Goodman, whose bullet-shattered bodies had just been found. At that service Bob Moses spoke from a pile of black rubble—all that was left of the Mount Zion Baptist Church, whose burning the three had gone to investigate. In this quiet, sunny glen, where all thought was directed to Mrs. Chaney, clad in black, mourning her teenage son, Moses surprised everyone by referring to a headline in that morning's paper which read: "President Johnson Says 'Shoot to Kill' in Gulf of Tonkin." Then he said: "This is what we're trying to do away with—the idea that whoever disagrees with us must be killed."

A year later, Moses was one of those arrested demonstrating in front of the Capitol in Washington against our Vietnam policy.

4. *The View from History: What Nation Can Be Trusted?*

HISTORIANS are probably more skeptical than other people about how much we can "learn from history," but I will offer a proposition which I believe modern history supports with a great deal of evidence: that no great power can be trusted—not Germany, Italy, Japan; not Russia, not France, not England, not the United States—when freedom and self-determination for other nations are at stake. All the great powers have at one time or another betrayed the desires of weaker nations, while accusing one another and persuading their own people of the justness of these accusations. We have been as gullible as citizens of other countries in believing the statements of leaders, and just as careless in neglecting to match these statements against the actual behavior of our nation.

Americans do not need proof of the iniquities of other nations. We recall England's empire, and her recent double-dealing with Israel and the Arab world: first wooing the Arabs by opposing Israel's independence, then joining Israel to act against Egypt's seizure of the Suez canal (the control of which by England was one of history's classic examples of imperialism). We remember Russia's cruel suppression of the Hungarian revolt. We know of France's savage fight to maintain her colony in Algeria.

But our memory somehow fails when it comes to our own history. Unlike some other nations, we do not burn our history books. The facts are available; it is just that we don't *see* them. We are not blind; but we have a defect of vision comparable to that of the color-blind person who, in one of those tests where he is asked to distinguish numbers in a mosaic of colors, cannot do so, although they are *there*.

This defect of vision is attributable to something found all over the world: call it nationalism, patriotism, chauvinism. For the United States this is aggravated by several special circumstances. We are a liberal nation with bountiful resources, a large and prosperous middle class, and a tradition of political pluralism and free expression; therefore we assume that such liberalism must be basic to our foreign affairs. (It was the false implication in Pericles' Funeral Oration, that a civilization so enlightened as that of Athens could not therefore pursue a selfish imperialism toward other states.) There is another factor: The experience of World War II overwhelms all that happened before and after; we still live in its atmosphere of total good confronting total evil, with *us* representing the good—and assume that all other conflicts can be measured with the same simplicity.

In addition there is the fact of widespread literacy, which has the unfortunate side effect of investing *words* with an importance so great that rhetoric can crowd out reality. Illiterate masses can be ignored or dealt with by force. Literate masses can be deceived, as all modern nations—whether called democratic or totalitarian—have shown. What is especially dangerous is that the leaders of nations begin to believe their own oratory. A self-deception which invests the entire leadership of a nation (including its intellectuals) with a powerful self-righteousness leads to sins which are uncalculated and therefore uncontrolled.

It is a matter of faith with most Americans that our policies in international relations are designed to further the values we cherish at home: liberty, justice, equality—the whole package of noble ideals expressed in the Declaration of Independence and the Bill of Rights, reiterated on thousands of occasions by our statesmen. The connection between national and international ideals has been compressed into a phrase: the free world. This phrase is repeated so frequently by our national leaders, our editorial writers, the mass media, that it is hardly questioned. It immediately links the freedoms already visible in America with all the actions of American foreign policy.

But are we dealing here with more than *words?* Have the values of liberty, justice, equality really been furthered by our *acts* of foreign policy since the end of World War II? This presumption is just not supported by the historical record.

I am not claiming that the behavior of the United States since the war has *always* violated these principles, only that it has done this so often, in so many areas of the world, that we must discard as a working hypothesis the idea that these values form the basis of American policy. Here is a short list of examples:

1. Support of French rule in Algeria against the demand of Algerians for independence. As one small piece of evidence, note the refusal of the United States to back a United Nations resolution, approved by the General Assembly's Political Committee on December 15, 1960, which asked for a United Nations-supervised plebiscite in Algeria.

2. Sustaining pashas and monarchs in the Middle East, in the midst of the most terrible poverty. For instance, the United States, through the C.I.A., plotted the overthrow of the nationalist Mossadegh in Iran in 1953, then backed the authoritarian rule of the Shah.

3. In Saudi Arabia the United States bolstered King Saud. *The New York Times* wrote, on the occasion of Saud's visit in January 1957: ". . . we naturally must feel critical of a regime that keeps its people in such misery and ignorance and even legalizes slavery. However, King Saud is our guest. . . . Saudi Arabia's oilfields are among the richest in the world, and they are being developed entirely by Americans. There is an American air base of importance at Dhahran, near the Persian Gulf."

4. In 1958, worried about a revolution in Iraq and about maintaining the status quo in neighboring Lebanon, the United States sent Marines into Lebanon. Hanson Baldwin, the *Times'* military expert, warned: "The Marines can, of course, maintain the existing Lebanese Government in power. . . . But their mere presence in Lebanon will be to Arab nationalists like a red flag to a bull." It seems pertinent to note that Lyndon Johnson, Democratic leader in the Senate at that time, pledged full support to Eisenhower, saying: "We will make it clear to the aggressors that this country is determined to maintain freedom in

this world at whatever the cost." There were no "aggressors" in Lebanon at this time—only Lebanese, and the United States Marines.

5. Underwriting of the Duvalier dictatorship in Haiti. On December 8, 1960, Camille Lherisson, a former Minister of Education and Health in Haiti, wrote a letter to *The New York Times,* noting the record of the Duvalier regime (which took power in October 1957 after rigged elections the month before) with its arrests, tortures, assassinations, students beaten to death, a thousand political prisoners in military barracks, expulsion from the Senate of six elected Senators and two justices of the Supreme Court: "Despite this situation, Duvalier so far has enjoyed the moral, economic, financial, and military support of the United States."

6. Failure to support independence for the remaining European colonies in Latin America. At the Inter-American Conference in Caracas in 1954, the United States was alone in refusing to request the elimination of European colonies in the Américas.

7. Actively helping to overthrow the legally elected Arbenz government in Guatemala in 1954, and then supporting the various dictatorships which succeeded it.

8. Friendly encouragement for the Trujillo dictatorship in the Dominican Republic, the Batista dictatorship in Cuba, the Branco dictatorship in Brazil, and the repressive regimes of Jimenez in Venezuela, Somoza in Nicaragua, Rivera in El Salvador. Herbert L. Matthews told the American Assembly on "Latin America and the United States" in 1959: "The United States failed to ride the tidal wave of democratic idealism that has been sweeping over Latin America in this decade. In fact, we often seemed to oppose it by favoritism to dictators."

9. Helping to keep in power the military dictatorship of General Stroessner in Paraguay since 1954. Stroessner used torture and imprisonment to hold down his opposition, and Canadian journalist Barry M. Lando wrote in *The Nation* (February 23, 1963): "For awhile the opposition parties in Paraguay believed that Alliance for Progress funds would be granted only to demo-

cratic regimes. Their belief is no longer as firm. Since July 1961, the United States has directly granted $10.5 million in aid to Paraguay and has participated in other grants worth $10 million."

10. Giving several billions in aid and arms to keep the corrupt dictatorship of Chiang Kai-shek in power on the Chinese mainland. Then, upon his retreat to Formosa, the United States remained silent as Chiang's men slaughtered from 5000 to 20,000 people (estimates vary; the higher figure is suggested by the new study of George Kerr, *Formosa Betrayed*).

11. Military and economic aid to Syngman Rhee in Korea (whose regime was comparable in its repressiveness to Chiang's) both before and after the Korean War. After Rhee's downfall in a coup in 1961, the United States supported other military strong men, notably General Park. *New York Times* correspondent A. M. Rosenthal wrote from Seoul, January 31, 1963: "Ever since the coup the United States has been working hard for the success of the *junta* Government. This was a calculated risk. It involved sacrificing the respect of some Koreans, who bitterly accused Washington of financing a dictatorship."

12. Repeated aid to the Portuguese dictatorship of Salazar, which has used torture and mass murder to maintain its rule over 4,000,000 Africans in its colony of Angola.

13. Military and economic assistance for Hitler's ally, General Franco, in Spain. Dean Rusk visited Spain in December 1965 to affirm American friendship.

14. Continuous refusal to put strong pressure on the racist regime in South Africa. In March 1966, a South African pro-government newspaper said it hoped that as new Undersecretary for African Affairs, the United States would appoint somebody "who will behave with the same responsibility in the field of relations between nations as the vast majority of American policy leaders such as Dean Rusk."

Let us now move closer to Vietnam by taking a brief look at the recent history of a neighbor, Laos. The Geneva Accords of 1954 provided for Laos to be a neutral state between pro-Western Thailand and Communist North Vietnam, and for the left-wing

Pathet Lao groups to be integrated into the country's political life. Almost immediately the United States began giving foreign aid, 80 percent of which went to build up the Laotian army for the purpose of eliminating the Pathet Lao. As Oliver E. Clubb, Jr., wrote in his detailed report for the Brookings Institution, *The United States and the Sino-Soviet Bloc in Southeast Asia:* "From the beginning of the American aid program until mid-1961, the struggle in Laos was characterized mainly by American-supported, right-wing efforts to stamp out the Pathet Lao and, concurrently, to maintain the right wing in power against neutralist opponents."

American aid enriched the Laotian elite, while the peasants remained poor; the pro-Western officials and merchants therefore began to lose support, and when it looked as if the next general elections would bring a popular victory for the Pathet Lao, the right wing moved to take power, renounced the Geneva Accords, and with U.S. support set up a military regime in late 1959. The result was a new upsurge in Pathet Lao guerrilla warfare, another coup, and neutralist Souvanna Phouma once more at the head, offering peace to the Pathet Lao and a cabinet post to the leader of the right wing, General Phoumi Nosavan. But again the United States worked against a neutralist solution, persuaded the general to reject the post, and then, against the advice of Britain and France, poured military aid into the general's forces for rebellion against the government, cutting off aid to the neutralist government. The general captured Vientiane in December 1960, and a new right-wing government was set up which immediately was given diplomatic recognition by the United States.

The effect of this was to bring the neutralists into alliance with the leftists and Soviet aid to the forces of the Pathet Lao. With the government based on rigged elections, corruption, and nepotism, the Pathet Lao—which had controlled only two provinces before—moved to take more than half the country. Kennedy in 1961 tried to get the approval of SEATO for military intervention against the Pathet Lao, but the SEATO Council, which had already during Eisenhower's administration rejected the American charge of "outside" aggression in Laos as a basis for intervention, would not go along.

At a new international conference in Switzerland in 1962, the United States, the Soviet Union, and the right, left, and neutral factions of Laos agreed on a neutralist government under Souvanna Phouma. The United States had continued to build up General Phoumi Nosavan's army, but it collapsed and fled before the Pathet Lao; now, with the only alternative a complete default to the Pathet Lao (and with Khrushchev still favoring a coalition government of the center), the United States put its weight behind agreement on a coalition government in June 1962.

What can we reasonably conclude from the experience in Laos?

(1) That we should be wary of official statements on Vietnam—because the same sincere assurances were given in Laos to a public that did not know what was happening until it was all over.

(2) That we ought to consider false until *proved* the claims that we are intervening in Vietnam because of outside aggression. In Laos (and this was affirmed by SEATO, our own creation) it was an *internal* revolt, and still we intervened.

(3) That we should be suspicious of the statement that we must support even an undemocratic ruler in order to fight Communism. In Laos military support for the local elite cost America the support of large numbers of non-Communists and ultimately strengthened Communism.

I have thrust very quickly into recent history because I believe that a judgment about our actions today depends heavily on the picture of the world we have in our heads before we even begin to think about the specifics of Vietnam. When we omit this history, myth rushes in to fill the spaces. And for the American public, this mytho-history consists of the statements of public officials, reiterated by the mass media, of what we *say* our foreign policy is—a policy based on the furtherance of "freedom."

To cut through the official words on Vietnam, we would need to study scrupulously American policy in action there. The alternative is to begin with a combination of noble presidential statements about our aims, accompanied by headlines about actions, which we then interpret in the soft glow of the stated aims. In 1927, President Coolidge, sending 5000 marines to Nicaragua to stop a revolution, said: "I am sure it is not the desire of the United States to intervene in the internal affairs of Nicaragua or of any other Central American republic. Nevertheless, it must be said that we have a very definite and special interest in the maintenance of order and good government in Nicaragua at the present time."

It is too easy to poke fun at Coolidge; the nature of governments remains the same. In 1955, Henry F. Holland, Assistant Secretary of State for Inter-American Affairs, said: ". . . we are firmly committed to the principle of nonintervention by one state in the internal affairs of another." (The C.I.A. had just succeeded in overthrowing the Guatemalan government.) Similar statements of innocence were uttered by U.S. officials at the time of the C.I.A. intervention in Indonesia in 1958, in deceiving the public about the U-2 affair in 1960, and in the 1961 invasion of Cuba.

Our ability to see reality through the web of official words is made more difficult when that web is spun by a liberal government which intersperses its generals with intellectuals. An item in *The New York Times,* November 25, 1965, read: "Arthur M. Schlesinger, Jr., said today he had lied to *The New York Times* in April 1961, about the nature and size of the Cuban refugee landing in the Bay of Pigs." Reminded by *The Times* that his statement of April 17, 1961, on the nature of the Bay of Pigs operation was contradicted by his book *A Thousand Days,* Schlesinger's response was: "Did I say that? Well I was lying. This was the cover story. I apologize. . . ."

Schlesinger's candor was laudable and rare. We should not be shocked—only brought to our senses. Governments do lie, and why should we ever have thought ours is an exception?

Our natural tendency—especially in a civilization so inundated with words and pictures—is to believe most firmly what we hear most often and to ignore the actions which flit like shadows across our consciousness at the same time. It thus becomes easy to accept the friendly assurance of a liberal, genial president: "We seek no wider war"—in the midst of a regular and speedy increase of troops (25,000 by July 1964; 54,000 by June 1965; 128,000 by September 1965; 300,000 by September 1966).

Without some record of past deeds, we might not search beyond the earnest statement by President Johnson at Johns Hopkins University, April 7, 1965, that the United States is ready for "unconditional" discussions with the enemy. But a group of scholars, examining the record (Schurmann, Scott, and Zelnik, *The Politics of Escalation in Vietnam*), found that in nine critical periods of the war there were moves by one or another party toward a negotiated settlement which were "retarded or broken off by American interventions, most of which have taken the form of military escalation." Consider again our natural longing for verbal assurance: the Schurmann study says that Johnson's speech at Johns Hopkins "represents a turning point in our official rhetoric" toward more emphasis on peace and negotiations, "but not, closer analysis suggests, any turning point in United States policy."

And so it is with some recollection of recent history that we turn to Vietnam itself.

5. The United States and Saigon: Reform or Revolution?

IT SEEMS that almost every great power has been involved in blocking Vietnamese independence in modern times. The French were the main culprit; they conquered Indochina around 1880 and maintained control through World War II. In 1940, the Vichy government, which collaborated with the Nazis after the fall of France, began to share power in Indochina with the invading Japanese. At this time the nationalist movement of the Vietminh was formed, carrying on guerrilla warfare against the French and the Japanese, under the leadership of Ho Chi Minh, a popular resistance leader and a Communist.

When the war ended in August 1945, Japanese power in Indochina collapsed. The Vietminh, taking over both in Saigon and Hanoi, issued a declaration of independence—an eloquent, passionate document, quoting from the American Declaration of Independence and the Declaration on the Rights of Man of the French Revolution. But at this very time the Big Three powers at Potsdam (England, the United States, the U.S.S.R.), in spite of all the grand wartime statements on self-determination, were deciding that Nationalist China would take temporary charge of Northern Vietnam and England would take over in the Southern half of the country. China was in no position to overturn the Vietminh power in the North, but in the South, a combination of English, French, and Japanese troops (see Harold Isaacs' account in *No Peace for Asia*) took over Saigon and restored French power.

In January 1946, the Vietminh held a national election, openly in their part of the country, secretly in the French part; it was the first general, popular election in the history of Indochina, and Ho Chi Minh became President of the Democratic

Republic of Vietnam. (Ellen Hammer, in *The Struggle for Indo-China*, describes this whole period in detail.) There was a kind of truce with the French, which soon fell apart in open conflict; the French shelled Haiphong, killing thousands, and there began in December 1946 the long war of France to maintain her colony.

And what was United States policy? In view of American claims today that its policy is to support self-determination and independence, the answer is both illuminating and troubling: The United States fully supported the French effort to maintain its power in Indochina against the nationalist struggle for independence.

When the French in 1949 set up Bao Dai (the former puppet Emperor who had abdicated power to Ho Chi Minh in 1945) as nominal head of state while they continued their war against the Vietminh, the United States immediately recognized Bao Dai. On June 27, 1950, President Truman announced that the United States would furnish military assistance for the war against the Vietminh. From then until 1954, the U.S. provided 80 percent of the cost of the war, sending the French a total of $2.5 billion. (See Robert Scheer's report to the Center for the Study of Democratic Institutions, *How the United States Got Involved in Vietnam.*)

None of this could save the French. What happened is summed up well by Edwin Reischauer in his 1954 book, *Wanted: An Asian Policy* (Reischauer could not predict then that his own country would later repeat the same mistakes, which he, as an Ambassador, would defend):

> Indochina is the classic case in which the Communists have utilized nationalism against us. There we find a sobering example of the weakness of defending the status quo against the offensive of Communist-dominated nationalism. In Indochina the French empire, the largest remaining traditional colonial power, backed by the financial and military resources of the United States, was pitted in a frustrating and at best indecisive battle against the Communist Vietminh.
> . . . in the realm of ideas the adherents of Vietminh were

on the offensive, while the French were engaged in a defense
of national pride and the fast dwindling residue of empire. . . . And in the economic field it was the Communists
who carried out much-needed land reform for the peasants.
. . . If we had had the foresight and the courage in the early
postwar years to persuade the French to extricate themselves
soon enough from their untenable position in Indochina,
the great force of Indochinese nationalism might not have
fallen into Communist hands.

The Geneva Conference of 1954, coming at the time of the
dramatic French defeat at Dienbienphu, salvaged something
for the puppet government of the French by assigning them
temporary control of Vietnam south of the 17th parallel, pend-
ing results of a nationwide election to be held in 1956. In the
meantime, the United States (mainly, Secretary of State Dulles
and Admiral Radford) had been trying to persuade England
to support a massive United States military attack on Vietnam
to save the French cause. But Eisenhower insisted he would not
do it without allied backing, and England would not go along.
Consequently, the United States half-heartedly accepted the Geneva settlements—not signing them, but issuing a separate declaration that it would "refrain from the threat or the use of force
to disturb them."

The United States did not at that time use "force to disturb
them" but it did something else. The heart of the Geneva Accords was the expectation of elections to unify the country by
July 1956. The United States, even while the meetings were
going on in Geneva, organized the Southeast Asia Treaty Or-
ganization. SEATO's membership consisted of three nations
not in Southeast Asia (the United States, France, England), two
white, Western-type nations in the Pacific (Australia, New Zea-
land), and three Asian countries dependent in various degrees
on United States economic and military aid (Thailand, the Philippines, Pakistan). As the French historian Philippe Devillers
wrote in "The Struggle for the Unification of Vietnam" (*China
Quarterly*, January-March 1962): "This was a pointer that the
United States would not sit by quietly if faced with the prospect

that South Vietnam might go Communist, even perhaps as a result of free elections."

The other move by the United States was to begin to throw its support to Ngo Dinh Diem, a former official in the French colonial government, whom Bao Dai picked as his new Premier while the Geneva discussions were going on. Devillers says: "As early as September 1954 it became clear that the Americans' desire to hold on to the 17th Parallel at all costs, would constitute a serious obstacle to the reunification of Vietnam . . ." In October 1954, a letter from President Eisenhower assured M. Diem of "the unconditional support of the United States." A year later Diem replaced Bao Dai as head of state. According to Devillers, North Vietnam, at least six times between 1956 and 1960, suggested to Diem a conference to plan elections on the basis of "free general elections by secret ballot," but each time it was rebuffed by Diem with United States approval (China and the Soviet Union protested, but without great force—another sign to the North Vietnamese that *no* great power really cared about a unified Vietnam).

Since 1954, when the Geneva Accords were drawn up, American soldiers have been in Vietnam—first in the hundreds, then in the thousands, now in the hundreds of thousands—to save whatever government was in power in Saigon. As Bernard Fall wrote in *The Two Viet-Nams*: "Without American aid to Viet-Nam's military and economic machinery, the country would not survive for ten minutes." If we withdraw, the Saigon government falls.

It is necessary then, as a first step, to see if that government, and our relationship to it, are worth saving. From 1954 until 1963, when he became a political liability, the United States gave military, economic, and moral support to Diem's regime. What kind of regime was this? A passage from Fall's book is instructive:

"Society," says Diem, "functions through personal relations among men at the top." Whether that image of history went out with Louis XIV is immaterial in the present context; that is the way Diem runs Viet-Nam. In such a *Weltanschauung,* compromise has no place and opposition of any kind must of necessity be subversive and must be suppressed with all the vigor the system is capable of. Thus, while South Viet-Nam is structurally a republic—mostly to please its American godfathers to whom that system is more familiar than any other—it is, in terms of the actual relations between government and governed, an absolute monarchy without a king, such as Admiral Horthy's Hungary was much of the time between the two World Wars, or as Franco's Spain has been since 1939.

Joseph Alsop, a firm defender of United States policy, called Saigon under Diem "a charming concentration camp." A minor illustration: Article 4 of the Morality Law read, "It is forbidden to dance anywhere at all." Bernard Fall commented: "The only similar instance I can recall occurred in Nazi-occupied Europe, where dancing was banned after Hitler's defeat at Stalingrad."

The Diem regime, constantly on the verge of collapse, was kept going by the United States with arms, money, and soldiers posing as "advisers." The regime was corrupt, unpopular, brutal —but there were endless promises of reform, both by the Diem regime and by top American officials who visited it regularly, returning with statements of hope.

Secretary of Defense Robert McNamara made his first visit to Vietnam in May of 1962; he said on his return that he had seen "nothing but progress and hopeful indications of further progress in the future." One year later, in May 1963, government troops opened fire on Buddhist demonstrators, killing eight; several monks set themselves afire. In November 1963, after military defeats and more Buddhist demonstrations, the Diem regime fell.

Two months later, January 30, 1964, it was replaced by a new military dictatorship. Major General Nguyen Khanh had seized power in a bloodless coup d'etat. Shortly after that, UPI correspondent Neil Sheehan reported the arrival in Saigon of Secretary of Defense McNamara "promising complete United States support for General Khanh and increases in military and economic aid."

Political repression continued under the succession of U.S.-

supported regimes that followed Diem. In May of 1964, for instance, General Khanh's government banned six newspapers and arrested nine political opponents accused of forming a political party without government permission. A UPI dispatch of May 24 reported that copies of one of the newspapers were seized because its first issue described General Khanh's regime as a "so-called democratic" government.

In June 1965, a military junta of ten generals took over South Vietnam, and Nguyen Cao Ky became Premier and spokesman for the group. Only one of these generals had fought for Vietnamese independence against the French. The others had either fought with the French or, like Ky, spent the war period being trained by the French.

The United States not only continued but sharply increased its military and economic support for the Ky regime, although that regime showed no improvement over its predecessors either in bringing economic reform to a harassed peasantry or in allowing free expression to the population. A Reuters dispatch from Saigon on October 17 described an order to the *Saigon Daily News* to halt publication for five days because it published articles without submitting them to the censor: "It was understood that an article by the syndicated American columnist Walter Lippmann displeased the government. The article published October 12 described the South Vietnamese army as war-weary and said it had too little morale to occupy territory that American forces seized from the Vietcong."

Ky was an embarrassment from the beginning, at one time even citing Hitler as a laudable example of strong government. The United States pretended not to notice. However, one American did. Early in 1966, Donald Duncan, a Master Sergeant of the United States Special Forces in Vietnam (the "Green Berets"), resigned from the army, saying ". . . anti-Communism is a lousy substitute for democracy." He reported that he and his fellows learned to use torture to extract information from Vietnamese. "We weren't preserving freedom. There was no freedom to preserve. To voice opposition to the government meant jail or death. Neutralism was forbidden or punished. We aren't the freedom fighters. We are the Russian tanks blasting the hopes of an Asian Hungary."

The United States continued to maintain that nothing serious was wrong. President Johnson summoned Ky to a meeting in Honolulu in early 1966; it ended in noble proclamations about mutual devotion, military victory, and social reform.

In the spring of 1966, Sgt. Duncan's point about "Hungary" turned out to be something of a prophecy. The dismissal of one of the generals of the junta precipitated a series of popular up-risings with a strong tone of anti-Americanism in Danang, Hue, and Saigon. These were led by Buddhist groups demanding the establishment of a civilian, democratic government. Tri Quang, a major Buddhist leader, called the Ky regime "rotten," indicated it was kept going only by American support, and said Ky's meeting with Johnson had only made him "more hated" by the average Vietnamese.

This was a revolt, but not an armed revolt. These were almost completely nonviolent demonstrations: students marching in Saigon, Hue, Danang, carrying placards, shouting slogans, in some cases taking over radio stations and government buildings. Whatever violence was done by the Buddhists was mostly on themselves: eight people burned themselves to death to protest against the Saigon government.

Many of the signs carried by the demonstrators indicated a strong desire to end the war, and one, carried in Saigon, read: "Foreign Countries Have No Right to Set Up Military Bases on Vietnamese Land." A wire service report from Saigon in April said:

> The chant "Da Dao My"—Down with Americans—echoed outside the fortified U.S. embassy where steel-helmeted Vietnamese troops faced a crowd of 7000 farmers in tattered clothing, dockworkers in conical hats, and white-shirted students.

For the United States this might have been an opportunity to end the war and still "save face" by maintaining neutrality during the rebellion. If the Buddhists had managed to create a new government, they might have negotiated for peace with the other side.

But the advice of the American government to the Ky government was clear: Stop the demonstrations by force. A *New York Times* dispatch of April 9, 1966 said that "Washington remains opposed to any transfer of power from the military to civilians at this time." The Ky government crushed the rebellion with rifles, machine-guns, and artillery, destroying pagodas and temples, killing civilian men, women, and children. American planes transported Ky's troops to Danang to deal with the dissidents. (*The New York Times* on April 5 carried a story from Washington: ". . . spokesmen at the White House, the State Department and the Defense Department would not confirm or deny reports that United States planes were helping the Saigon Government to fly its troops to Danang." Alongside this was a dispatch from Danang, saying that "in response to a request, the United States had provided some of the transport aircraft that brought the Government troops to Danang.")

The rebellion was suppressed successfully. A minor postscript was added on August 31, 1966, in a news story from Saigon:

> The United States has suspended its program of assistance to the University of Hue, which was a major command post for the Buddhist-led dissidence that swept Central Vietnam earlier this year.
>
> Responsible sources said that the step had been taken because the embassy is determined to have nothing to do with the university until it starts functioning again as an educational institution instead of a political clubhouse.

Once again, history was manufactured—subtly, the way it is done by a liberal society. The facts of the rebellion all appeared in the newspapers, and anyone already dubious about the Saigon government could put them all together. But how could most Americans be suspicious, when the heads of the government had just returned happily from the Pacific—Johnson from Honolulu, Humphrey from Saigon—proclaiming that all was well, that Ky "talks just like Tugwell" (as the President put it), that a great program of social and economic reform was under way? And who would take the trouble to assemble all the dispatches and then put them alongside the history of previous regimes in Saigon? It was easier to listen to CBS News which, reporting the Saigon demonstrations on March 30, said: ". . . once again, the forces of anarchy are on the move in Saigon."

James Reston, however, was one to put it all together, even as the demonstrations began, on April 3:

> The basis of American intervention in the beginning—and even of the official American thesis now—is that we are in Saigon to support a "Government" and a "nation" against external aggression, which that Government and nation must win or lose primarily by themselves; but there is no Saigon Government that can govern, and no South Vietnamese "nation" in our understanding of the word. . . .
>
> So Washington is in trouble. It is relying on myths and the only consolation of the present political demonstrations is that they are at least exposing the reality.

It was a brief exposure. A mammoth, busy society, blinking from too much television, could miss it.

How can American support for such governments be justified? To some it hardly needs justification; anything is preferable to Communism—even a dictatorship based on a wealthy elite controlling impoverished masses. American liberals, however, cannot accept this, not at first; they must seek a third way, so that our foreign policy can satisfy the aims of liberty and justice, and the rest. What they refuse to grasp is that where a third way is indeed feasible, it cannot be manufactured and exported like Coca-Cola; groups within the nation must find and further this third way as groups found such ways—on their own—in Yugoslavia, Burma, Cambodia, Kenya, Ghana, Egypt, Scandinavia. Without such indigenous power a third way cannot be imposed. Refusing to accept these limits to what an outsider can do, the United States engages in a giant pretense; it announces that reform is on the way, then it entrusts the carrying out of that reform to those very people who constitute the right-wing elites of wealth—those who have most to lose by change.

And so American liberal presidents and vice-presidents have justified their support for a succession of right-wing dictators and juntas in Vietnam by promising, again and again, social and economic reforms. (We forget that after a certain point in 1775, no talk of liberal reform *under the crown* was acceptable; the colonists just had to have a clean sweep—a revolutionary change.) From Diem to Ky, reforms were asked, promised, ignored, then promised again—and each time with that pleasant amnesia that cannot recall what happened before.

Any move toward reform must start with the fact that Vietnam is a land of peasants, and the fundamental problem of the nation is the problem of the peasant: how to have enough land without burdensome payments to a landlord or heavy taxes to a corrupt government; and how to have peace and security to farm that land and take care of a family. That problem was not solved under the French; it has not been solved since. In North Vietnam, most of the land traditionally consisted of small holdings; but in South Vietnam, about 6000 landlords (most of them absentee) owned, and still own, about 2.5 million acres of rice land. Thus 2 percent of the landowners hold 45 percent of the land. Most of the peasants have tiny holdings, and over 500,000 have no land at all.

The Diem regime's "land reform" was too slow, too puny, and had too many loopholes. For instance, the government ostentatiously announced that no one could henceforth own over 250 acres, but large rubber, tea, sugarcane, cocoa plantations were exempt. By contrast, when much of South Vietnam was occupied by the Vietminh before the Geneva Accords, they administered a much more effective land reform program. As John D. Montgomery, in *The Politics of Foreign Aid*, wrote: "The early implementation of land reform under the Diem regime was somewhat apathetic by comparison with what the Communists had promised and in part carried out."

Bernard Fall notes that between 1957 and 1960, the Diem regime built 6500 square meters of hospitals, 86,000 square meters of schools, and 425,000 square meters of high-rent villas and apartment buildings. Fall adds: "That is the sort of thing—far

more than weapons and infiltrators from across the 17th parallel
—that makes Communist guerrillas out of peaceable peasants."

When the Ky regime took power in 1965, the promises began
to flow again; forgotten was the history of Diem, who had had
almost *ten years* in which to achieve reform, with pitiable results.
The lapse of memory in the United States was born of political
necessity; by now the level of our military activity was enormous—a liberal Democratic administration had to persuade
the nation that all these billions, all these lives, were going
for *something*. Thus in February 1966, President Johnson, having
met Ky in Honolulu, talked grandly about social reform;
Humphrey, back from Saigon, bubbled about a "social revolution." The Vice-President's exuberance seemed to depress Tom
Wicker of *The New York Times*, who wrote from Saigon:

> Against the palpable background of Vietcong power, of
> Saigon's lack of popular support in the countryside and of
> the immense task of reforming Vietnamese society, some offi-
> cials here and many resident foreigners suggested that Mr.
> Humphrey's statements, coming after the Declaration of Hon-
> olulu, were an example of political overkill.

The emphasis on social reform, Wicker said, was to "quiet
critics." He pointed out that before leaving Saigon, Humphrey
produced members of American aid teams who gave reporters
glowing reports on reform programs. But listeners "were disturbed by what they considered propaganda about programs
they knew at first hand, and about reform efforts that they believe are in infancy."

Liberals have puzzled and worried over this and a dozen situa-
tions like this: They don't like dictatorships; they would like
social reform; what, oh what, can the United States do? There
is an answer, but it is outside the accepted list of alternatives;
this is a problem which, by its nature, cannot be solved by the
United States with its present psychology. South Vietnam has
needed a social revolution. Revolutions anyplace are genuine
only when they are carried on by the people of that place. Such
revolutions, in the circumstances of the undeveloped world,
will be led by groups on the left which the United States,

without a sharp change in its thinking, is not disposed to help.

So the self-deception continues. (The "Alliance for Progress" in Latin America is another example.) Liberal presidents and vice-presidents proclaim that "reform" will be administered by dictators and plutocrats. The result is that American statesmen who are "liberals" at home will sustain a state of terror abroad by surrounding it with the promise of change. The change then turns out to be spurious and picayune, but the devastation which accompanies it is not at all spurious and is dealt out on a grand scale.

On January 24, 1966, a dispatch in the *Washington Star* by reporter Richard Critchfield illustrated, as clearly as any one story could, the social problem which remained unsolved in Vietnam after twenty years of war by Frenchmen and Americans, against Communist-led nationalists:

> In Long An, one of Vietnam's most fertile provinces, more then 85 percent of the peasant population are tenants. This land-ownership pattern may help explain why, despite a tremendous cost in lives and material, the war in Long An is no closer to being won than it was several years ago. . . .
>
> Most important in Long An, however, government and the mass of peasantry still seem to be on the opposing sides. Land is of such paramount importance here that the Viet Cong allow only the landless or very poor farmers to command guerrilla units or qualify as party members. The provincial government's social order is the exact reverse. Most of the military officers, civil servants and community leaders come from the land-owning generals. The same is true in Saigon where only one of the 10 generals now sharing power has any rapport with the masses. He is Central Vietnam's erratic Maj. Gen. Nguyen Chanh Thi, who also is the only one of peasant origin. . . . [It was this general who was soon to be dismissed by the Ky junta, bringing on the Buddhist uprising.]
>
> In the delta, out of 1.2 million farms, only 260,000 are owner-operated. . . . Some 3,000 rich Saigon families still are the big landowners.

In February 1966, on the eve of the outbreaks, *New York Times* reporter Charles Mohr (who previously was forced to leave *Time* because his candid articles from Vietnam were displeasing to the editors) wrote a revealing article from the village of Trucgiang. He reported that some Americans working in the countryside believed "nothing short of major changes in the country's social system" could produce conditions leading to military victory. Mohr pointed out that in South Vietnam, a second baccalaureate degree is a virtual necessity to become an army officer or government official. "Yet it can be obtained in almost all cases only by the children of the privileged classes, which already control Vietnamese society and like it that way." A young AID officer told Mohr: "It is still virtually impossible for a child born in a poor rural family to obtain a baccalaureate degree, without which he is permanently relegated to an inferior social position. . . . To these children the Vietcong offers the only real outlet for their energy."

Mohr referred to the many stories in the American press and speeches by administration leaders, offering encouragement and telling of imminent reform in South Vietnam, of defections from the Vietcong. "But, despite many speeches, there is not yet an indication of change in the fundamental system. . . . Almost no Vietcong leaders defect, apparently because they know that they cannot find any meaningful, dignified place in South Vietnamese society. The Vietcong movement makes use of the native shrewdness and leadership capability of the peasant, but the Government will not because he has no degree."

Pointing to Johnson's pledge at Honolulu to give economic aid, Mohr wrote: ". . . in the view of some experienced American officials, aid is not enough" because "few of these efforts upset in any way the established system. . . . For the outcast . . . the rules have to be changed, and until they are, he has no choice but to go on fighting for a change."

Neil Sheehan wrote in *The New York Times* (October 9, 1966) after three years as correspondent in Vietnam:

> While there are some patriotic and decent individuals among them, most of the men who rule Saigon have, like the Bourbons, learned nothing and forgotten nothing. They seek to retain what privileges they have and to regain those they have lost.

In Vietnam, only the Communists represent revolution and

social change, for better or worse according to a man's politics. . . .

It seems clear that the billions of dollars, the tens of thousands
of lives lost in Vietnam, cannot be justified by what we are doing
for social change there. Assuming that our basic bundle of values
consists of life and liberty, we might agree that sometimes liberty may be sacrificed for life, or life for liberty. But if we are
giving up *both*, then nothing is left in the bundle. And if so,
then we had better withdraw from the scene.

The "realists" may take the argument one step further and
say: *Both* life and liberty must be sacrificed in one area of the
globe in order to safeguard both in others. We might accept
this if we were without the record of recent United States foreign
policy, which shows that we have been supporting dictatorships
in a dozen other countries—in Europe, Africa, the Middle East,
Latin America, the Far East. When it is demanded ten, fifteen,
twenty times—indeed, most of the time—that life and liberty
both be sacrificed to an end which is still not in sight, then we
may become suspicious.

Until Vietnam, we have mainly been helping others—whether
imperial powers, as France in Algeria, Portugal in Angola; or
local tyrants, such as Trujillo, Saud, Duvalier—in the double
sacrifice of life and liberty. Now we are doing it ourselves, engaging in a direct military assault on the population of Vietnam,
its countryside, its cities. With the French gone, our allies aloof,
the local government inept, Uncle Sam, the white-gloved finan-
cier of counterrevolution, has removed his gloves, taken gun in
hand, and moved into the jungle.

If there is social gain in this action, we have no evidence of
it in the nature of the government we are upholding in Vietnam. Perhaps there are other, larger social gains involved; we
will later consider this. But in any event, such gains will need
to be measured against the present human cost. We should, therefore, take a look at this cost—that is, at the scale and kind of
violence going on in Vietnam. Because ultimately, we must
weigh the presumed evil consequences of withdrawing against
the immediate acts now taking place.

6. *Violence: The Moral Equation*

WORLD WAR II was almost over when my squadron of B-17s was sent to bomb a small encampment of German soldiers near Bordeaux. The Allies had retaken France and were across the Rhine; these Germans, left behind, were simply waiting for the war to end. We seemed to be running out of targets and were told at our briefing that this mission was testing a new kind of bomb— jellied gasoline (now called napalm). So we destroyed the German encampment. Our bombs fell also on a little French town nearby, called Royan. It was set afire and many of its inhabitants died in the flames.

I don't remember having any hesitation about releasing those fire-bombs. And since that day I have never doubted that all of us are capable of the most atrocious acts—not because our intent is evil, but because it is so good. We set laudable ultimate goals, and these enable us to proceed to the most ruthless acts without scrupulously making sure they lead to those goals.

One of the outstanding falsehoods of the cold war, repeated endlessly to school children and the lay public, is that the chief difference between us and the Communists lies in their willingness to "use any means to gain their ends." Considering that war is as extreme a means as has been devised, and that *all* great nations engage in it, then the United States must be included as a nation which, like the others, will use any means to gain its ends.

Let us, for example, look at some of the means being used in Vietnam by this liberal nation:

1. From *The New York Times*, August 3, 1965:
   The Marines burned huts they believed were the sites of sniper fire. A sergeant said orders called for this. . . . United States Marines found a woman and two children among 25

persons they killed . . . perhaps from one of the 1000 artillery shells poured into the area. . . . A grenade hurled by a Marine blasted two children to death in an air-raid shelter.

2. The *Washington Post,* March 13, 1965, said American pilots "are given a square marked on a map and told to hit every hamlet within the area. The pilots know they sometimes are bombing women and children."

3. Stephen Cary of the American Friends Service Committee reported in *The Progressive,* October 1965, his conversation with a United States official who had been the first to enter a village after an American air strike, and who said: "I could take everything but the dead kids. As a matter of fact I found only two persons alive—a boy of ten and his eight-year-old sister. They were sitting quietly on the ruins of their house, surrounded by the bodies of their mother and father and several other children."

4. A *Reuters* dispatch, March 18, 1965: "Planes bombed a nearby village yesterday, killing about 45 villagers, including 37 school children . . ." An air strike by United States Skyraiders had been ordered after Vietcong were reported in the vicinity.

5. Malcolm Browne, in *The New Face of War:*
    In the last week of September, 1964, an intelligence report reached a province headquarters in the Mekong Delta that thirty sampans loaded with Viet Cong troops were moving down a nearby canal. . . . A flight of A-1H fighters found the thirty sampans with no difficulty, and the whole run was duck soup. Within fifteen minutes, every sampan had been blown to matchwood. . . . A trigger-happy field intelligence agent had seen and correctly counted the sampans but his guess as to what was in them was not correct. They were all civilians, most of them women and children. Twenty-seven were killed and thirty seriously injured. The Air Force announced blandly that it would take steps to avoid a recurrence of such accidents. But similar announcements have been made after many of the hundreds or thousands of such incidents in the past, and basically nothing changes. . . .

6. A dispatch by Jack Langguth in *The New York Times,* June 5, 1965, from Saigon:

As the Communists withdrew from Quangngai last Monday, United States jet bombers pounded the hills into which they were headed. Many Vietnamese—one estimate is as high as 500—were killed by the strikes. The American contention is that they were Vietcong soldiers. But three out of four patients seeking treatment in a Vietnamese hospital afterward for burns from napalm, or jellied gasoline, were village women.

7. Charles Mohr reported from Saigon, August 30, 1965, in *The New York Times:*

The military command, which has been conscious of criticism of the B-52 raids, has apparently concluded that saturation bombing of suspected Vietcong "safe havens" is a profitable military operation. . . . A qualified source said he had verified reports that civilians moved out of the area of a raid in Zone D last Thursday because they could not stand the smell of decomposing bodies, indicating that sizable casualties had been inflicted by the bombs.

8. A UPI dispatch, August 3, 1965, from Chan Son:

"I got me a VC, man. I got at least two of them bastards." The exultant cry followed a 10-second burst of automatic-weapons fire yesterday, and the dull crump of a grenade exploding underground. The Marines ordered a Vietnamese corporal to go down into the grenade-blasted hole to pull out their victims. The victims were three children between 11 and 14—two boys and a girl. Their bodies were riddled with bullets. . . . "Oh, my God," a young Marine exclaimed. "They're all kids."

9. A story in *The New York Times,* August 5, 1965, from Saigon:

A United States military spokesman outlined today for the first time some of the combat rules set down for American Marines fighting in South Vietnam. . . . "Marines do not burn houses or villages unless those houses or villages are fortified," he said.

When a reporter remarked that a great majority of the

villages in Vietnam were fortified to some degree, the spokesman looked up from the text and said, "I know it."

10. Charles Mohr in *The New York Times,* from Saigon, September 5, 1965:

In Bien Hoa province south of Saigon on August 15 United States aircraft accidentally bombed a Buddhist pagoda and a Catholic church . . . it was the third time their pagoda had been bombed in 1965. A temple of the Cao Dai religious sect in the same area has been bombed twice this year.

In another delta province there is a woman who has both arms burned off by napalm and her eyelids so badly burned that she cannot close them. When it is time for her to sleep her family puts a blanket over her head. The woman had two of her children killed in the air strike that maimed her.

Few Americans appreciate what their nation is doing to South Vietnam with airpower . . . this is strategic bombing in a friendly allied country . . . innocent civilians are dying every day in South Vietnam.

11. A *New York Herald Tribune* article from Saigon, September 11, 1965:

United States Air Force B-52 jet bombers . . . dropped hundreds of tons of high explosives on the hamlet of Phuong X Tay. . . . The raid had been ordered after intelligence experts concluded the hamlet to be a large Communist communications center. But . . . what aerial photoanalysts thought were sandbagged bunkers appeared to be an ancient wall. What had appeared to be fortified trenches turned out to be seldom-used oxcart trails.

12. Neil Sheehan in *The New York Times,* November 30, 1965:

Duchai is on the central Vietnamese coast, north of Saigon. Last May its complex of five prosperous fishing hamlets, set among fruit groves and palm trees behind a spacious beach, was occupied by Vietcong guerillas.

In mid-August, United States and Vietnamese military officials decided the Communists were using Duchai as a base for the operations in the area and that it should be destroyed.

For the next two months, until the Vietcong finally withdrew in mid-October and Duchai was reoccupied by Government troops, it was periodically and ferociously shelled by Seventh Fleet destroyers and bombed by Vietnamese and American planes.

Vietnamese Government officials are certain that at least 184 civilians died during Duchai's two months of agony, but . . . no one really knows how many civilians were killed. Some reasonable estimates run as high as 600. . . .

"There," said a fisherman, pointing to a bomb crater beside a ruined house, "a woman and her six children were killed in a bomb shelter when it got a direct hit."

Duchai's solid brick and stucco houses, the product of generations of hard-earned savings by its fishermen, were reduced to rubble or blasted into skeletons. . . . Here and there napalm blackened the ruins. . . .

At least 10 other hamlets in this heavily populated province of about 700,000 persons . . . have been destroyed as thoroughly as the five in Duchai.

At least 25 other hamlets have been heavily damaged. . . .

Each month 600 to 1000 civilians wounded by bombs, shells, bullets and napalm are brought to the provincial hospital. . . . Officials say that about 30 per cent of these cases required major surgery. A recent visitor to the hospital found several children lying on cots under mosquito netting, their bodies horribly burned by napalm.

13. On November 1, 1965, *I. F. Stone's Weekly* carried a story from *Paris-Match* about a French priest, Father Currien, who told the fate of his church and the villagers caught in a bombing. There had been a battle in the vicinity between Vietcong and government forces. Then:

"We were left alone. No one was in the village except for some women, children and old people. . . . I heard some planes. The first bomb fell at 6:05 on my church. There was nothing left of it. I ran for shelter to the presbytery, a wooden house adjoining the church. A second bomb crushed it and I was pinned under the beams. Children cried, women shrieked, and the wounded moaned. . . . I made the women and children lie down under the flooring of the house. There we passed the entire night while those accursed planes hammered with rockets and bombs at my village.

"Next morning . . . I buried as best I could the bodies of my faithful. I remember now I buried seven of them completely torn to bits. I had to abandon some wounded and dying. . . .

"I have seen my faithful burned up in napalm. I have seen the bodies of women and children blown to bits. I have seen all my villages razed. My God, it's not possible! . . .

"When I arrived in Saigon, I could barely drag myself along. Two Americans wanted to give me a lift to the hospital in their automobile. I couldn't stand it. Always before my eyes were those burned-up women and children. I told them to get the H——— out because I didn't like murderers. They were probably nice guys who wanted to help me. In Saigon they probably pound away at typewriters in an air-conditioned office and know nothing of this war. They couldn't understand what was the matter with me."

14. In *The New York Times,* from Saigon, November 8, 1965:
    For the second time in 10 days American planes bombed a friendly South Vietnamese village by mistake yesterday. . . . One woman was killed and ten other civilians were wounded. . . . Newsmen had been told repeatedly that no tactical strikes are made in South Vietnam unless an air controller is hovering over the target in a light plane, but a senior Air Force officer said tonight that some raids using radar were regularly carried out on a "blind" basis. . . .

    In the October 30 bombing, in the village of Beduc, 48 persons were killed and 55 were injured by two United States Air Force A-1E Skyraiders.

15. A *New York Times* headline over a story from Saigon, November 13, 1965: "United States Investigates Bombing Mistake. South Vietnamese Killed in 3d Error in 8 Weeks."

16. In the *Boston Globe,* sometime in 1965:
    Marines, combing the village for its inhabitants, peered,

gun in hand, into holes in the ground. Some villagers were dragged out of underground hideouts. Terror etched their faces. Women wailed and clutched half-naked infants. . . . Marines shouted to their Vietnamese interpreter to tell the villagers not to be afraid. Three women were injured by a fragmentation grenade which a Marine dropped into one tunnel. One woman suffered the loss of an eye.

17. Bernard Fall reported in *Ramparts,* December 1965, on his ride in a Skyraider over a fishing village:

The napalm was expected to force the people—fearing the heat and the burning—out into the open. Then the second plane was to move in with heavy fragmentation bombs to hit whatever—or whomever—had rushed out into the open. . . . We came down very low, flying very fast, and I could see some of the villagers trying to head away from the burning shore in their sampans. The village was burning fiercely. . . . There were probably between 1000 and 1500 people living in the fishing village we attacked. It is difficult to estimate how many were killed. It is equally difficult to judge if there actually were any Viet Cong in the village, and if so, if any were killed.

18. An AP dispatch from Washington, January 6, 1966:

The head of the United States medical aid program in South Vietnam said Wednesday the war is causing more casualties to civilians than to soldiers because of the nature of the war.

19. *Newsweek,* August 22, 1966:

Truong Thanh's troubles began when the Vietnamese province chief heard that a company of Viet Cong was sheltering in the village—which has long been guerrilla-dominated. Better than risk a bloody ground battle, the province chief called for a United States air strike. His request was approved by both United States and Vietnamese authorities, and early one evening an American spotter plane flew over Truong Thanh to mark the target with a smoke bomb. Moments later, two F-100 Super Sabres flashed in, spitting 20 mm. cannon fire and showering the village with napalm and bombs. By the time the Super Sabres made their last pass, sixteen Truong Thanh residents, including six chil-

dren, were dead and 124 lay wounded. . . . Asked if it were
true that under present United States military ground rules
in Vietnam, incidents such as occurred at Truong Thanh
were apt to happen again, the United States provincial ad-
viser replied: "Honestly, there is that probability."

20. Neil Sheehan, writing in *The New York Times,* February
14, 1966:
  . . . within three hamlets, about 1000 peasant homes have
been blasted apart by bombs and shells or incinerated by
napalm. . . . In the village of Tamquan . . . at least 100
civilians are estimated to have been killed. One distraught
woman appeared at a field medical station holding a child
whose legs had been horribly burned by napalm. The child
is not expected to live.

21. Eric Pace, reporting in *The New York Times,* July 3, 1966,
from Tanuyen:
  United States Air Force lawyers made condolence payments of 33 piasters (about 30 cents) this week-end to each
of the families of seven children killed accidentally Friday
by an Air Force weapon. . . .

22. Thich Nhat Hanh, director of the School of Social Studies
at the Buddhist University of Saigon, told students at
Harvard University in May 1966, that since the Vietcong
were indistinguishable from the peasants, there was a high
rate of civilian casualties. "When your press reports that
600 Cong were killed in a military operation, that figure
may include 590 innocent peasants."

23. An article in the *Honolulu Advertiser,* August 24, 1966,
by the paper's reporter in Saigon:
  Nothing so tragically points up the problem of the air
war in the South as the way United States Air Force jets
bombed and strafed a Delta hamlet near Can Tho, killing
or wounding more than 100 civilians.
  Indications are such things happen far more often than
officials like to admit. . . .

24. The *Japan Times,* August 16, 1966, carried an AP dispatch from Saigon:

Two more apparently mistaken bombings of Vietnamese villages came to light Monday to bring to four the number of such incidents since last Tuesday.

25. A UPI dispatch from Saigon, August 23, 1966:
The Saigon Post reported today that 30 civilians were killed and 30 others wounded last week when jet planes strafed a river barge convoy near Saigon. . . . The newspaper did not identify the jets, but said they strafed scores of barges, mistakenly identifying them as Viet Cong–operated vessels.

26. In Tokyo, August 1966, I heard five Americans (Kay Boyle, the novelist; Russell Johnson of the American Friends Service Committee; Sgt. Donald Duncan; Floyd McKissick of CORE; Rabbi Israel Dresner) tell of their visit to a Cambodian border village on August first, the day after it was strafed by United States helicopters flying very low over the houses. A pregnant woman, running for cover, was machine-gunned to death; the Americans saw her body in one of the huts. Two children were drowned in a ditch trying to escape. The group of Americans left, and the following day, August second, more United States planes came over and the village was completely destroyed.

These twenty-six items are not exceptions but examples. They are not isolated events; United States planes fly over a thousand sorties each week, dealing out death to people they cannot identify as friend or foe. This list, then, is only a tiny *known* part of an enormous pattern of devastation which, if seen in its entirety, would have to be described as one of the most evil acts committed by any nation in modern times.

We have been deceived repeatedly by Johnson, Humphrey, Rusk, McNamara, and the rest on the matter of the killing of civilians. They have continually given comforting assurances that "military" targets are chosen. But we ought to keep in mind that when the bombing of a village is explained apologetically as an "accident," the accident is not that a village was bombed, but that the *wrong* village was bombed. The women and children of village A are killed, regretfully, because someone *thought* shots came out of the village. The women and children of village B are killed, without regrets, because shots *did* come out of the village.

The Cambodian incidents, where we had five eyewitnesses, is instructive. Even after the administration reversed itself on which country the village was in, it could still not refrain from lying just a little. According to the *Asahi Evening News* in Japan, August 13, 1966: "Meanwhile, the United States Mission in Saigon today issued a communique expressing deep regret at the machine-gunning of targets near the Cambodian village of Thok Trak on July 31 and on August 2." A woman in the village was cut down and the village huts were destroyed, but the communique said targets "near" the village were attacked.

More important, however, is that the government's "deep regret" was because the village was Cambodian. If United States helicopters had flown low over a Vietnamese village a few miles across the border, killed a woman, and set fire to the villagers' homes, there would have been no cause for regret; that would have been a normal military operation.

Historical perspective is sobering. When the Japanese bombed Shanghai, when the Italians bombed Addis Ababa, when Fascist planes bombed Guernica, when the Nazis bombed Warsaw, Coventry, London—the civilized world reacted with horror. Never in history had the defenseless civilian populations of cities been the object of deliberate bombing attacks. It was not just that the Axis powers' *ends* were wrong. It was that the bombing of cities was a barbarous act which by its nature could have no justification. Yet during World War II, we killed 50,000 in Hamburg in one terrible night of fire-bombs, and 80,000 in Tokyo in another nightmare of terror, and then hundreds of thousands with the atom bombs on Hiroshima and Nagasaki.

Now we are at it again. But with this difference: In World War II it was a terrible mistake in judgment. We could have made a distinction between the violence necessary to defeat Hitler's armies and that which was inflicted on civilian populations. The bombings were superfluous to the war and could have been eliminated (the Russians defeated the Nazi armies using only tactical aircraft against soldiers and not engaging in strategic bombing against cities). *In Vietnam, however, the bombing and shelling of civilians constitutes the war.*

This has a huge implication. The only way we can stop the mass killing of civilians—of women and children—is to stop the war itself. We have grown accustomed to the distinction between "ordinary" acts of war and "atrocities," and so came a whole host of international conventions setting up rules for mass slaughter. It was a gigantic fraud, enabling the normal horror of war to be accepted if unaccompanied by "atrocities." The Vietnam war, by its nature, does not permit this distinction. In Vietnam, the war *itself* is an atrocity.

Since the killing of civilians is inevitable in our military actions in Vietnam, it cannot be called an "accident" on the ground that nobody *intends* to kill civilians. The B-52 crews, the Marines and GI's moving through the villages, don't *plan* to kill civilians, but when bombs are dropped on fishing villages and sampans, when grenades are dropped down tunnels, when artillery is poured into a hamlet, when no one can tell the difference between a farmer and a Vietcong and the verdict is guilty until proved innocent, then the mass killing of civilians is inevitable. It is not deliberate. But neither is it an accident. It is not *part* of the war and so discardable. It *is* the war.

As correspondents have often said, the Vietcong are indistinguishable from any Vietnamese peasant. Indeed, they *are* Vietnamese peasants. This is guerrilla warfare, in the countryside, and the guerrillas are part of that countryside. Most of them live there. That is exactly why the United States is bombing villages, inundating whole areas with bombs, destroying rice fields, spreading chemicals and fire over huge sections of South Vietnam—which we claim to be defending.

All this is obscured by the terminology of the war, which plays on the long history of cold-war symbolism in the United States. Somehow, when the headlines read "400 Communists Slain" we do not get the feeling that these are Vietnamese farmers who have been killed, but rather *objects* which deserve to be destroyed. When the news stories tell of the bodies of "Vietcong" littering the field after an attack, few Americans feel compassion; the Vietcong is the "enemy"—a word which has no human content. When *The New York Times* reports (as it did February 14, 1966) that in one action 986 "guerrillas" were killed and 161 weapons found in the vicinity, then one wonders about those 825 "guerrillas" who were unarmed.

Many people are aghast at the mass killing of innocents, even angrily comparing the United States to Nazi Germany. Indeed, the West Germans have referred to American troops in Vietnam as *Bandenkampf-verbande* (Bandit Fighting Units), which was the name given during World War II to the Waffen-SS groups which specialized in killing guerrillas and their families.

Liberal Americans, even those critical of the war, are often offended by this analogy. Johnson is *not* Hitler; the United States is *not* Germany; there is no act we have committed which is comparable to the calm, organized annihilation of six million Jews. And yet, would it not be an enormous disservice to the memory of those six million if their fate should henceforth become a device for excusing every *lesser* act of mass murder? Hitler so extended the boundaries of the possible that any actions less extreme than his—no matter how horrible—can be tolerated.

It cannot lessen our guilt in Vietnam to speak of violence on the other side. Even if the Vietcong killed their fellow countrymen as massively, as indiscriminately as does the United States, that would create no moral justification for our doing the same. They have, indeed, committed certain indefensible acts: placing land mines, throwing grenades, planting bombs, in places where noncombatants become the victims. But does our large-scale bombing of the countryside prevent such behavior—or does it rather intensify the righteous anger of a revolutionary group, raise the level of warfare, and thus escalate irrational acts on both sides?

The fact is, however, that the Vietcong are not killing in as large numbers or as indiscriminately as we are. Our own statistics prove this. We have reported consistently that their casualties are far greater than ours. If they were twice ours, and if only half of these were civilians, it would mean we have been killing more civilians than the total number of people killed by the other side. To use the figures given by our military and our press, their casualties are four times ours, and at least 80 percent of these are civilians; so we are killing three times as many *civilians* as they are killing in all. This is to be expected. They use small arms and field pieces; we use heavy artillery and huge bombers.

President Johnson and his aides have often responded to criticism of large-scale American bombardment by referring to the Vietcong's killing of government officials. Several thousand officials (no one knows exactly how many) on the provincial, district, and village levels have been assassinated by the guerrillas. It hardly seems necessary to argue that the destruction of a village's *population* cannot be justified by the fact that the other side kills a village's officials. Foreign correspondent Max Clos, writing in *Le Figaro Literaire,* March 3, 1965 (quoted in Marvin Gettleman's excellent collection of documents, *Vietnam)* writes of the Vietcong assassinations:

> . . . The chief of the province appointed by the Saigon Government lives in a big house, drives a Mercedes, and loads his wife with jewelry. The Governor is a man of importance who is approached with deference, protected by police, soldiers, and assistants. His Vietcong opposite number can be seen every day. He is out among the people. He is dressed like a peasant, in black calico and with sandals cut from an old tire. He makes his rounds in his district on foot, walking along the public roads. You can be sure of one thing: He is not getting rich on the back of the people.
>
> When the Vietcong began their revolution in 1959 and 1960, it was opened with a wave of terrorism. In isolated places, in hamlets, then in villages and cities, officials and private persons loyal to Saigon were assassinated. Government propaganda strove mightily to exploit these facts to arouse popular indignation. This backfired. It was understood too late that in most cases the peasants had fearlessly helped in the brutal liquidation of the men on whose death the Saigon Government was basing its case. Instead of murderers the terrorists were considered dispensers of justice.

Early in 1966, Senator Robert Kennedy made a speech to the International Police Academy. One of the passages in the prepared text was never delivered. It read: "Air attacks by a government on its own villages are likely to be far more dangerous and costly to the people than is the individual and selective terrorism of an insurgent movement."

The Vietcong's acts of terrorism will need some powerful reason to justify them. But the discussion would have to begin by noting that their violence is focused far more accurately on those they blame for the plight of the country than is ours on the people we hold responsible.

Violence as a means of achieving social change is a very complex problem. An absolute position of nonviolence is logically hard to defend, it seems to me. If people are ruled by a powerful and unrelenting oppressor, nonviolence might compel them to forego social change. They would thus be condemned to a permanent cruelty that might be ended by a violent but brief rebellion.

There is, in other words, always the theoretical possibility that a small violence may be required to prevent a larger one. I would cite three kinds of examples: the removal of a malignant tumor by surgery; the possible assassination of Hitler to shorten World War II; the action of a Negro mother, alone with her children, whose home in Georgia was about to be invaded by a mob of armed white men, and who fired her shotgun through the door, killing one and dispersing the rest.

Yet the rationalization of violence is so easy and so frequent that once we give up a position of absolute nonviolence, the door is open to the most shocking abuses. Therefore, our starting point should always be the premise that violence is to be avoided and other methods of achieving change should be sought.

If violence is ever to be justified, the evidence must be overwhelming and clear; the greater the proposed violence the greater must be both the magnitude of the social goal and the certainty that it will be achieved. Certain other principles are also essential: that the more closely the violence is focused on the social malignancy—as in precision surgery—the greater likelihood that it can be justified; that the persons who pay the price (since cost must be measured against gain) are the ones who decide whether violence will be used. Self-defense, involving direct action by the persons attacked and against the attacker, meets both these principles.

Modern warfare has certain fundamental characteristics which make it the least defensible use of violence in achieving any social goals: It is massive, indiscriminate, not focused on the evil-doers; its human cost is gigantic; it violates the principle of free choice on two counts, because it is fought by conscripts, and against people who did not decide to be involved (civilians).

Revolution within a country, on the other hand, is by its nature focused against the regime presumed to be oppressive. It involves self-determination, because revolutionaries, not having total state power, cannot create conscript armies; they depend on the consent of the oppressed. Guerrilla warfare especially is both focused and voluntaristic.

The United States, not engaged in a war where it is defending itself against direct attack, claims it is helping another people defend themselves. This claim will be discussed later. At this point, however, simply because of the scale and nature of the violence in Vietnam, certain conclusions are possible, whether or not the United States is fighting "against aggression," whether or not the cause of the Vietcong is that of a just revolutionary upheaval:

(1) Our morality is not the inverse of theirs. Even if our claim were true that we are defending the South Vietnamese against aggression from "the outside," there can be no justification in carrying on a military action which kills most of the people we claim to be defending.

(2) If, however, the claim of "defense" is not true, and the Vietcong are conducting a geniune struggle for independence and social change, then the United States has crossed the Pacific to put down a revolutionary movement. And in so doing it is indiscriminately destroying not only the insurgents themselves, but the population as a whole: their homes, their land, their roads, their boats, their forests, their cities.

In either case, therefore, the continuation of the present American violence in Vietnam is one of the cruelest acts of an age which is marked by its cruelty. The daily toll in Vietnam of innocent people is so terrible that the cessation of our military activity—the bombings, the burning and shelling of villages, the search-and-destroy operations—has become no longer debatable or negotiable, but a matter of urgent and unilateral action.

Two major arguments remain. One says that while we may stop or diminish our offensive activity, we should maintain a military presence in South Vietnam to support a South Vietnamese government which *is* fighting, not a counterrevolutionary war, but a defensive war against outside aggressors. The other argument says that even if it *is* a counterrevolutionary rather than a defensive war we are fighting, and even if we are killing innocent Vietnamese on a large scale, we must continue our military actions—even increase them—because a gigantic issue is at stake which requires this sacrifice: Communism vs. freedom.

These arguments will be studied in the next two chapters.

7. *A Double Deception:*
The Problem of Aggression

THIS CHAPTER intends to examine the statement given most frequently by the United States government to the American public as the chief reason for our military action in Vietnam: that we are fighting to defeat "aggression from the North." I will try to show that (1) the conflict is not fundamentally due to "aggression from the North," and (2) the government itself does not believe that this is the reason the United States is in Vietnam. There are two official deceptions involved: the first as to the nature of the war, the second as to the nature of American foreign policy.

In his opening statement of January 28, 1966, before the Senate Foreign Relations Committee, Secretary of State Dean Rusk said: "The heart of the problem in South Vietnam is the effort of North Vietnam to impose its will by force. For that purpose Hanoi has infiltrated into South Vietnam large quantities of arms and tens of thousands of trained and armed men, including units of the North Vietnamese regular army. It is that external aggression, which the North has repeatedly escalated, that is responsible for the presence of United States combat forces." And again in that testimony: "The United States has a clear and direct commitment to the security of South Vietnam against external attack." And again: ". . . we shall do what is necessary to assist the South Vietnamese to repel the aggression against them."

Senator Fulbright was politely suspicious as he began one of those duels in which men of state speak to one another, elliptically, each knowing exactly what is on the other's mind, but never exposing the issue with such clarity that the mass public can really understand—a discussion, in other words, antithetical to democracy and typical of high-level diplomacy.

Fulbright: Could you tell us very briefly, when did we first become involved in Vietnam?

Rusk: That began 1949–1950, Mr. Chairman. . . .

Fulbright: Was France at that time trying to reassert her colonial domination of Vietnam? Was that her objective at that time?

Rusk replied, without answering that question, becoming more muddy as he went along. So that the reader can judge, here is his reply:

> I think just at the conclusion of the war, in that part of the world, the first step that was taken was the restoration of the status quo ante bellum in the broadest sense in India, Burma, Malaysia, Indochina, Indonesia, and indeed in part in the Philippines, although the Philippines moved almost immediately for independence. In varying degrees each of these areas became independent from the former colonial country, and in different circumstances.
>
> In the case of France, the first step that was made was to work out something like a commonwealth arrangement, associated states in which France would retain certain authority with respect to defense and foreign affairs. But there was never a firm basis of agreement among most of the Indochinese people themselves; and that moved—it proceeded inevitably and I think properly, toward a more clear independence.

Fulbright did not challenge in Rusk's evasion the false statement of fact on the "first step" of France. (Actually, the "first step" of France was to try a direct military recapture of her former colony, what Jean Lacouture calls "the colonial expedition"; only when this failed did she try a more indirect form of control through the puppet Bao Dai.) And Fulbright did not say bluntly to Rusk that he had not replied to the question; he simply *assumed* that Rusk had answered the question in the affirmative, and went on from there.

> Fulbright: . . . but what moved the State Department of our government to assist France to retain her control of Vietnam . . . ?

Rusk: The problem there, sir, was—I am trying my best to remember something which happened quite a few years ago— the problem was not just that, or was not at all that really of assisting France and establishing and reinforcing a colonial position, but to give France a chance to work out its political settlement with these states on the basis of their own independence, and without having Communism as a basic—without giving to the Communists a basic position in Southeast Asia. . . .

Fulbright courteously refrained from a further discussion of France's aims—everybody in the world but Dean Rusk seemed to know that France's aim was precisely "establishing and reinforcing a colonial position." And he did not dissect the double American intention Rusk spoke of (independence *and* avoidance of Communism) by pointing out that this was at the time an impossible task since the leader of the independence movement in Vietnam was also the leader of the Vietnamese Communists: Ho Chi Minh. He went on instead to discuss the extent of United States aid ("I think it was approximately $2 billion," Rusk said) and other matters.

What was implicit in Fulbright's questioning was this: If "external aggression" was the reason for United States intervention, then why had the United States intervened (not with men, because France had 600,000 in Vietnam, but by bearing the main expenses of maintaining those 600,000 French troops) at a time when there was no North and South Vietnam, when there was clearly no "external" aggression, when it was the French vs. the Vietminh in a faintly disguised colonial war?

Rusk was, to put it in nonacademic language, "snowing" the American public, which in the main does not know the history of U.S. involvement in Indochina (indeed, Rusk himself was "trying my best to remember"), but millions of whom were watching the telecast of those hearings. And while there was some clever questioning of Rusk, there was not the kind of direct confrontation of falsehood with truth which people in a democracy deserve to have in the interrogation of government leaders.

Support for the French colonial war had started under Truman and continued under Eisenhower. Eisenhower, in a letter to Winston Churchill of April 4, 1954 (reproduced in Eisenhower's book *Mandate for Change*) wrote:

> Dear Winston: I am sure . . . you are following with the deepest interest and anxiety the daily reports of the gallant fight being put up by the French at Dien Bien Phu. . . . I fear that the French cannot alone see the thing through. . . . And if they do not see it through and Indochina passes into the hands of the Communists the ultimate effect on our and your global strategic position with the consequent shift in the power ratios throughout Asia and the Pacific could be disastrous, and, I know, unacceptable to you and me. . . .

Eisenhower was not talking to the public, but to an ally. He was explaining American support for the French not in any moral terms, like defeating "aggression," but in terms of "global strategic position" and "power ratios." Whatever the validity of Eisenhower's analysis he was candid. Shortly after this letter, Dulles proposed massive American military action to support the French.

It was very clear to all sides, in those years when the United States began its intervention in Indochina, that there was only one party engaging in "external aggression" and "external attack" in Vietnam: the French. And the United States was helping the French, massively, to reestablish control over a former colony. This simple fact of recent history—and this is what Fulbright was getting at in his opening questions—casts huge doubt, to put it moderately, on the administration's claims today that its major reason for being in Vietnam is to "repel the aggression."

From 1950 to 1954, the United States was giving aid to the aggressor in Vietnam. Can anyone with some recollection of recent history believe that if the Vietcong were about to win in South Vietnam—without *any* aid from anywhere else—the United States would keep hands off? Did we keep hands off in other cases where there was clearly no outside aggression—in Guatemala, in Cuba, in the Dominican Republic? Indeed, in Vietnam itself, as we shall see later, the United States had already landed 23,000 combat troops when the infiltration from the

North was only a trickle and consisted almost entirely of Southerners.

But Rusk had an enormous television audience watching. And he said:

> If the infiltration of men and arms from the North were not in the picture, these troops of ours could come home; we have said that repeatedly. They went in there, the combat troops went in there because of infiltration of men and arms from the North, and that is the simple and elementary basis for the presence of American combat forces. . . .

Senator Frank Church of Idaho was not satisfied with Rusk's explanation. If it was only the presence of "foreign" soldiers (assuming the North Vietnamese to be "foreign") that caused the American military presence, then why were American troops stationed in South Korea? The following exchange took place:

> Church: How many American troops are now stationed in South Korea?
> Rusk: In South Korea, I think it is approximately 55,000.
> Church: It has been twelve years now, roughly, since the truce, is that correct?
> Rusk: Yes, sir, that is correct.
> Church: How many Chinese combat troops are stationed in North Korea?
> Rusk: I think there are no Chinese there at present. . . .
> Church: Very well. We presently have 200,000 American troops in South Vietnam. Indications are that the buildup is going to continue. . . . Supposing that whatever the requirement may turn out to be, our military concentration, our American buildup of military forces in South Vietnam, is finally sufficient to suppress the Vietcong, and to pacify South Vietnam. Would you then think that it is likely to be any easier for us to withdraw from South Vietnam than it has been for us to withdraw from South Korea?
> Rusk: . . . Indeed, the only reason for their presence is the infiltration of men and arms from North Vietnam. So the answer to your question would turn on what North Vietnam's conduct and attitude is.

Church: But North Korea hasn't been engaging in that kind of activity in South Korea for many years, has it?
Rusk: No, but you will recall—
Church: But our troops are still in South Korea.

Rusk then did not respond directly to what Church was saying. He simply went on for some length about the history of events in Korea, how a withdrawal there had led to a miscalculation, and then said: "I don't know what the future will hold on this particular point. It would depend a good deal on the general orientation, attitude, and posture of Peking. . . ."

What Church had succeeded in eliciting from Rusk was an indirect admission (but not easy for a television audience to follow carefully) that we maintained military forces in Asian countries *not* because of "aggression," but simply because of the *presence* of China on the Asian continent.

If, as Rusk said, "infiltration of men and arms from the North . . . is the simple and elementary basis for the presence of American combat forces," then it became important to determine how large a part men and arms "from the North" played in the Vietcong operations. Senator Pell questioned Rusk on this:

Pell: As I understand, there are about a quarter of a million Vietcong. What portion of those would be from North Vietnam?
Rusk: . . . I would suppose that 80 percent of those who are called Vietcong are or have been Southerners. . . .
Pell: . . . but would it be a fact that the United States forces in South Vietnam would be about four times the number of those born in North Vietnam who are with the Vietcong and there would be no Chinese in South Vietnam?

Rusk did not respond to Pell's point about the U.S. forces greatly outnumbering the North Vietnamese in South Vietnam; he confined his response to reiterating the point about no Chinese in South Vietnam. Pell did not press Rusk on this comparison of North Vietnamese and American "outsiders," but said:

This question of whether it is a Vietnamese war or an American war is one that concerns us here. . . . The more you read about it, the more you realize it is really one country, one people, one basic language with various divisions . . . so we have to determine how much of this is a civil war and how much is not.

Later on in the hearings, Senator Church rekindled this issue by pointing to the American Civil War, where the North did actually invade the South, and yet it was called a civil war. Then he said:

> . . . Now, in Vietnam you can look at the war in Vietnam as a covert invasion of the South by the North or you can look at it as some other scholars do, as basically an indigenous war in which the North has given a growing measure of aid and abetment; but either way you look at it it is a war between Vietnamese to determine what the ultimate kind of government is going to be for Vietnam. When I went to school, that was a civil war. . . .

Senator Church's point is crucial, because if it is valid, then the entire government case on "aggression" is demolished. Civil wars and revolutionary wars always involve "aggression" by one side or the other. However, this may be morally justified, as in a revolution against an oppressive regime, or a civil war to end slavery. The use of the term "aggression" to capture American public support for the war in Vietnam invokes a moral principle which has had enormous emotional appeal since the rise of Hitler: that no *nation* should cross the borders of another *nation* to try to take it over.

Vietnam is not only in fact "one country, one people," as Senator Pell said, but this unity was recognized in the Geneva Agreements of 1954, which the United States did not sign, but promised to uphold. The Final Declaration of the Geneva Accords, in Point 6, provided: ". . . the military demarcation line [the 17th parallel, the line dividing North and South Vietnam] is provisional and should not in any way be interpreted as constituting a political or territorial boundary." So we find the United States first backing Diem in his rejection of unification talks in 1956, and then using the continued separation of North and South as a basis for charging "aggression."

If Vietnam is one country, then no matter how many North Vietnamese are fighting in South Vietnam, they are still Vietnamese, whereas the Americans are not. That would make it a civil war, and not the kind of "aggression" officials have been talking about to justify the American military presence.

Even, however, if North Vietnam and South Vietnam are separate countries, the government has yet to prove its contention that North Vietnam is fundamentally responsible for what appears to be a revolution in the South against an unpopular regime, fighting for several years with local people and local weapons and only beginning to get aid from the North after the United States entered the war in force. On this question, the weight of evidence by scholars and observers is overwhelming:

1. Philippe Devillers, the French historian, author of the standard work on the early stages of the war, *Histoire du Vietnam 1945–1951* (writing in *The China Quarterly*, January-March 1962):

> The point of view of most foreign governments, in the West especially, is that the fighting going on in South Vietnam is simply a subversive campaign directed from Hanoi. The hypothesis is certainly a plausible one . . . but it leaves out of account the fact that the insurrection existed before the Communists decided to take part, and that they were simply forced to join in. And even among the Communists, the initiative did not originate in Hanoi, but from the grass roots, where the people were literally driven by Diem to take up arms in self-defense.

2. Bernard Fall, in *The Two Viet-Nams,* referred to a speech by Walt Rostow in which Rostow said: ". . . the operation run from Hanoi against Viet-Nam is as certain a form of aggression as the violation of the 38th parallel by the North Korean armies in June, 1950." Fall commented:

> . . . one might dismiss it as merely another one of those commencement addresses that most speakers prefer history to forget. But it illustrates the muddled thinking of high Administration officials: The . . . assertion—that North Viet-

namese infiltration into South Viet-Nam is the direct equivalent of the North Korean invasion of the ROK—omits the embarrassing fact that anti-Diem guerrillas were active long before infiltrated North Vietnamese elements joined the fray.

3. Jean Lacouture, in *Vietnam Between Two Truces,* writes:

. . . Hanoi claims that it is not intervening in the South, and Washington insists that the battle in the South is an invasion, while in reality it is a rebellion which originated locally but which Hanoi has increasingly supplied. The war originated in the South and is being waged and suffered by the South, although with growing participation by the North.

4. Donald S. Zagoria, a Columbia University specialist on Asian Communism, wrote *(Commentary,* February 1965):

Although the Vietcong does unquestionably get valuable help, training, and assistance from North Vietnam, it is reasonably clear that we are dealing with an indigenous insurrection in the South, and that this, not Northern assistance, is the main trouble.

5. David Halberstam, Vietnam correspondent for *The New York Times,* writing in that newspaper October 27, 1963:

Although much of the articulation for their war and their tactics and their trained cadres comes from Hanoi, this is primarily an indigenous war. The Vietcong manpower is locally recruited.

6. Robert Scigliano, who worked with Michigan State University's Vietnam Advisory Group, a government-connected project in South Vietnam, wrote in *South Vietnam: Nation Under Stress* (1964):

Only a small portion of the Communist military units and agents operating within the Republic of Vietnam has been sent from North Vietnam, and nearly all of these have been Southerners who withdrew to the North after the Geneva Agreements. . . . The South Vietnamese government's claim of massive infiltration does not appear to be supported by the available evidence. . . . Similarly, most of the weapons and other supplies available to the Communist forces in the South have been obtained there. . . .

State Department "proof" of Northern aggression rests heavily on the fact that the creation of the National Liberation Front of South Vietnam was approved by the Third National Congress of the Lao Dong (Workers Party) of North Vietnam which met in Hanoi in September 1960. Scigliano talks about the revolt being "launched" and "directed" from North Vietnam, even while saying that Southern men and materials were the basic ingredients of this revolt. Political scientist Robert Scalapino, at the National Teach-In on May 15, 1965 in Washington, said that the Communist Party of South Vietnam, numbering 500, "could not be expected to dominate the 500,000-man Party of the North." (But it didn't have to *dominate* the Lao Dong; all it had to do was participate in the initiation of guerrilla action in the South.)

What the State Department omits from its account, Jean Lacouture reports in his book: that one year before the Hanoi Congress—that is, in 1959—as a result of fraudulent elections, witch-hunts, jailings under the Diem regime, "a guerrilla force began to operate which was probably the first sign of the reactivation of Communist organisms." This was in the northern provinces of South Vietnam. In other places, "at the periphery of the Plain of Joncs, or in the Transbassac or in the Ben Cat region north of the capital, subversive groups fighting the regime had a primarily nationalist or religious orientation." Then, six months before the Hanoi Congress, in March 1960, there came "the actual birth of the National Liberation Front" when "a group of the old resistance fighters assembled in Zone D, issued a proclamation calling the prevailing situation 'intolerable' for the people as a result of Diem's actions, and called upon patriots to regroup with a view toward ultimate collective action."

Lacouture makes it clear that, far from the Hanoi government's having initiated the rebellion, it had problems of its own and wanted to keep things quiet for a while, but it was pressured by the Southern victims of the Diem regime to at least declare itself on the need for a revolt. The Party Congress in Hanoi did not issue its statement, Lacouture says, "except at the specific demand and under the moral pressure of the militants in the South, who criticized their Northern comrades' relative passivity in the face of the repression exercised against them by the Saigon authorities. . . ."

The historian Devillers goes into greater detail in his article "The Struggle for the Unification of Vietnam" in *The China Quarterly* (referred to above). He traces the revolt back to Diem's "manhunts" in 1957, roundups in 1958 ("A certain sequence of events became almost classical: denunciation, encirclement of villages, searches and raids, arrest of suspects, plundering, interrogations enlivened sometimes by torture . . ."), leading to the start of guerrilla warfare in 1959, and the official establishment of the NLF in December 1960 in the South. He makes it clear that not just Communists, but many non-Communist nationalist elements, were preparing for revolution against the Diem regime; he also refers to the *reluctance* of North Vietnam to become involved.

The United States government's charges of "aggression from the North" simply cannot stand up under examination, and only the general public's impatience with dates and figures enables the deception to be perpetuated for so long. According to the Department of State publication, *Aggression from the North,* 1800 men had infiltrated into South Vietnam from the North by 1960. At this time the United States already had 4000 military in South Vietnam. The State Department claims another 3700 infiltrated in 1961. But in that year, the United States added far more (6000, according to the Mansfield report; 11,000 according to Lacouture). And those "infiltrees" were not only Vietnamese, but they were mostly South Vietnamese returning home to join a revolution begun by fellow Southerners. In 1961 when, according to the State Department, there were a total of 4500 infiltrees from the North, President Kennedy accepted the General Staff recommendation to begin sending 40,000 troops to Vietnam.

Indeed, as late as the Spring of 1964, whatever infiltrees there were coming down were apparently still mainly or wholly

Southerners, and most Vietcong weapons were still of local origin. On March 6, 1964, David Halberstam wrote in *The New York Times*: "The war is largely a conflict of Southerners fought on Southern land. No capture of North Vietnamese in the South has come to light, and it is generally believed that most Vietcong weapons have been seized from the South Vietnamese forces." At this time, the United States had at least 23,000 troops in South Vietnam. (The Geneva Accords limited the United States to 685 men, and Johnson in his 1965 State of the Union Address declared that the United States "would stand by the Geneva Agreements of 1954.")

In early 1965 the State Department issued a *White Paper* to document its charges of "aggression from the North." This was so quickly and thoroughly demolished by I. F. Stone's careful appraisal that it was hardly referred to again by administration spokesmen. Its charts and figures *looked* impressive, but when one did all the necessary counting, it turned out to have little substance. The White Paper claimed 19,550 infiltrees from 1959 to 1964, but it could only actually cite 23 infiltrees, and a check of the provinces these were born in indicates that only six were Northerners. Stone showed that the 179 captured Vietcong weapons listed by the White Paper as having come from Communist countries outside Vietnam were about 2 percent of the total number of weapons captured.

After Senator Mansfield's committee visited Vietnam it reported to the Committee on Foreign Relations in January 1966 that there were 14,000 North Vietnamese regular troops out of a total Vietcong strength of 230,000—that is, about 6 percent. At this time, there were 170,000 United States troops in Vietnam, or more than ten times the number of North Vietnamese. Indeed, there were in South Vietnam more troops from South Korea (21,000) than from North Vietnam, according to the Mansfield Report.

What was clear by 1966, when United States troops totaled 300,000, is that the United States had taken over the bulk of military operations from the South Vietnamese government, while the Vietcong, though receiving more help from North Vietnam, remained overwhelmingly a guerrilla army of Southerners. A *New York Times* dispatch of March 2, 1966, said that the flow of supplies to the Vietcong from North Vietnam had been averaging 12 to 30 tons a day, while the United States was moving, every day, 24,000 tons of supplies by ship alone "plus an undisclosed amount by air."

To use the relatively small amount of aid given the Vietcong by North Vietnam, or the weapons now increasingly coming to them from Communist countries, as evidence of "outside aggression" would be to deny the whole history of revolutions, which almost always have received help from the outside. Without French military aid, the American revolution might not have succeeded. Ninety percent of the gunpowder used by the colonists in the first few months of the war came from abroad. The culminating victory of the Revolutionary War at Yorktown was due in large part to the French fleet under Admiral de Grasse, and to 7800 French troops joining the 9000 Americans. On July 2, 1957, John F. Kennedy (speaking on the Senate floor about the revolution in Algeria) said: "Most political revolutions, including our own, have been buoyed by outside aid in men, weapons, and ideas."

The indigenous strength of the Vietcong is no longer open to serious dispute (the Mansfield Report shows that from 1962 to 1965, when 14,000 North Vietnamese joined the fray, over 100,000 men joined from the South). What is in doubt today is the indigenous nature of the force attempting to put down the Vietcong. During the Diem regime, and perhaps for two years after that, it could be said that South Vietnamese government forces, although equipped and financed almost entirely by the United States and augmented by American troops, were trying to defeat the Vietcong guerrillas. But they were failing. The hollowness of the South Vietnam government became more and more apparent. Its large conscripted army would not fight. A news dispatch of January 1965 indicated that 30 percent of the government's draftees deserted in six weeks. Over 100,000 deserted in the year 1965. The regime, unlike the guerrillas, did not have popular support.

By 1966, with American casualties exceeding South Vietnamese government casualties, with American planes filling the skies, with American equipment pouring in, with 300,000 United States troops engaging in most of the offensive operations, with $2 billion spent each month to conduct the war—and with the Ky regime tottering, able to stave off rebellion only in a brutal show of force abetted by the United States—this had become an American war. The South Vietnamese knew this. The demonstrations that took place in Saigon, Danang, Hue, were anti-American, with banners: "Americans Must Cease Interfering in Vietnamese Affairs" and "Stop Killing Our People." *The New York Times* reported on April 23, 1966 "resentment of the United States presence in many areas of South Vietnam."

The evidence points to a conclusion most Americans find distasteful: that the United States, by 1966, had taken on the French burden in Vietnam and, with a shadow government as a front, was putting down a nationalist-Communist revolution with the classic ferocity of a Western imperial power. Almost everybody in the world but Americans could see that, whatever the character of the Vietcong, they were Vietnamese, while the Americans, destroying land and people on a frightening scale, were the only ones who matched the accusation of "outside aggression."

Neither the history of events in South Vietnam nor the history of American policy outside South Vietnam supports the argument that the defeat of "aggression" is the reason for the U.S. military presence there. But it is an appealing one for presentation to mass television audiences. The administration does not really expect to deceive the informed minority in the country with this argument, just as it does not really expect them to believe that we are fighting for "freedom" in defending the Ky government, its predecessors and its successors. These are perimeter defenses, intended to discourage all but the truly obstinate questioners. When these are breached, then the officialdom falls back on the kind of argument that Dean Rusk gave to the House Foreign Affairs Committee, August 3, 1965: "The loss of Southeast Asia to the Communists would constitute a serious shift in the balance of power against the interests of the free world. And the loss of South Vietnam would make the defense of the rest of Southeast Asia much more costly and difficult." (Robert Scigliano reports, in *South Vietnam: Nation Under Stress*: "As American officials are wont to say in nonpublic pronouncements, Vietnam is a piece of real estate that must be held by the West.")

The United States government really doesn't care very much about "aggression from the North." It doesn't care deeply about "freedom" in South Vietnam. It doesn't care whether or not the revolution conducted by the guerrillas of the Vietcong is indigenous or not, idealistic or not, popular or not. What it does care about is that this revolution is a *Communist* revolution, which threatens to bring about, at the least, a Communist-dominated South Vietnam, or—more likely—a unified Communist Vietnam.

While the United States sometimes refers to this among other reasons, it does not like to put the problem so boldly and simply, even though almost all Americans are anti-Communist, because a fearful thing is implied: that wherever there is a Communist revolution imminent anywhere in the world (and there are a number of countries where such a revolution could break out), the United States feels driven to take whatever action is necessary to prevent it or destroy it. And this makes of us what Rusk told the Foreign Relations Committee we would *not* be: "the gendarmes of the universe."

It is not *just* that 12 million more people would live under-Communist rule. How serious a change can that be in a world where a billion people already live under such rule? And there is no persuasive evidence to indicate that the Vietnamese would be worse off under Ho Chi Minh that they have been under Diem or Ky; indeed, the lower classes—and most Vietnamese are peasants—would probably be better off. As Neil Sheehan, a troubled supporter of the American presence, wrote on returning from three years in Vietnam as a *New York Times* correspondent: "In Vietnam, only the Communists represent revolution and social change, for better or worse according to a man's politics."

The problem, Rusk and Johnson and McNamara and both Bundys have said, is that a Communist Vietnam would (as Rusk put it) "constitute a serious shift in the balance of power." Not because of the shift in the tiny country of Vietnam. But because, as Johnson said at Johns Hopkins: "Let no one think for a moment that retreat from Vietnam would bring an end to conflict. The battle would be renewed in one country and then another." A Communist Vietnam would lead to a Communist Southeast Asia. A Communist Southeast Asia would lead to Communism developing in other parts of the world. And this would lead, as Rusk suggested in a speech of April 23, 1965, to the American Society of International Law, "to the eventual communization of the entire world."

This is the argument, often referred to as the "domino theory" or the "Munich analogy," that we need to examine now, because in one form or another it is accepted not only by Administration supporters; it is also accepted by many who believe we should halt our damaging offensive actions in Vietnam, while retaining our military presence there. It is, then, the chief argument against complete military withdrawal.

8. *Munich, Dominos, and Containment*

AT WHAT POINT deception turns into self-deception is impossible to say, and so it seems pointless to try to reconstruct the "intent" or the "sincerity" of officials (in any of the world's governments) or to say how *consciously* they are thinking and moving along a certain line. Each single act in a series may be clearly conscious, while the total direction of the behavior is only vaguely sensed. When an outsider reconstructs the "thinking" of statesmen as forming a certain pattern, he is imposing an order which is rarely preconceived, and yet may be enormously important in its implications. With this warning, I want to speculate a bit on the psychological origin of the "Munich analogy" used by the President and others to justify the United States military action in Vietnam.

The analogy comes first, I would suggest, out of a need to pile up more and more reasons to persuade the public, because it is evident that the public has been in great need of persuasion. (This administration watches the polls closely; in September 1966, the Harris Poll showed that less than half the population approved Johnson's handling of the Vietnam war.) The various reasons given for the Vietnam war partly overlap, are partly distinct—saving freedom in South Vietnam, fighting aggression, stopping Communism. If one doesn't quite persuade, the speaker moves on to the next one. The supposition is that three unconvincing arguments may add up to one strong one.

Each succeeding argument comes closer and closer to what postwar history shows to be the core principle of United States foreign policy: that somehow, we must "stop Communism." This belief is not questioned or examined; it has become a matter of faith. It does not come from a rational study of Communism in its complexities and contradictions, its changes over time, its move from monolith to bipolarity to multipolarity. It is not informed by the work on Communism produced by the nation's scholars. We have here a reflex action, conditioned over a long period of time, so that any warning of "Communism," however faint or uncertain, brings a violent response. (An Ambassador sends an urgent dispatch from Santo Domingo saying that "Communists"—who later turned out to be largely mythical—are about to take over the government, and the Marines are on their way.)

It is part of the psychology of collective man or, as Niebuhr put it, of "immoral society," which insists on drawing chalk lines on the globe to separate good and bad, friend and foe, failing to recognize that no such geopolitical division can do justice to the complexity of good and evil in the world. It is George Orwell's *Animal Farm*, where "everyone on two legs is our enemy; everyone on four legs is our friend." It is almost exactly the psychology of Colonel Cathcart in *Catch-22*, where everything that happened in the world was measured by a simple test: "Will this give me a black eye, or will it put a feather in my cap?" Our national leaders now have the habit of judging every international development this way: Will it spread Communism, or stop it?

There is one American official who has understood this psychology, but his advice goes unheeded. George Kennan wrote in *Russia and the West Under Lenin and Stalin*:

> There is, let me assure you, nothing in nature more egocentrical than the embattled democracy. It soon becomes the victim of its own war propaganda. It then tends to attach to its own cause an absolute value which distorts its own vision on everything else. Its enemy becomes the embodiment of all evil. Its own side, on the other hand, is the center of all virtue. The contest comes to be viewed as having a final, apocalyptic quality. If we lose, all is lost; life will no longer be worth living; there will be nothing to be salvaged. If we win, then everything will be possible; all problems will become soluble; the one great source of evil—*our* enemy—will have been

crushed; the forces of good will then sweep forward unimpeded; all worthy aspirations will be satisfied.

The leaders of the United States have worked themselves and the citizenry of the country into this apocalyptic view of world affairs: If Vietnam goes Communist, all is lost—if not now, soon. Yet the facts of Vietnam, the pictures on television, the growing criticism by respected public figures, have for the first time since World War II created some doubts. An effort involving hundreds of thousands of soldiers and billions of dollars needs powerful, unquestionable reasons, and these are hard to find in the visible facts of the Vietnam case.

But there is at hand a one-piece substitute that comes prefabricated with its own rationale, surrounded by an emotional aura strong enough to ward off inspectors. This is the Munich analogy which, transplanted to Vietnam, speaks with all the passion of Churchill in the Battle of Britain, declaring that to surrender in Vietnam is to do what Chamberlain did at Munich—that is why the villagers must die. As Johnson said (July 28, 1965):

> If we are driven from the field in Vietnam, then no nation can ever again have the same confidence in American promises, or in American protection. In each land, the forces of independence would be considerably weakened. And an Asia so threatened by Communist domination would imperil the security of the United States itself. . . .
>
> We learned from Hitler at Munich that success only feeds the appetite of aggression. The battle would be renewed in one country and then another, bringing with it perhaps even larger and crueler conflict. . . .

One of the great values of the Munich analogy to the Strangeloves is that it captures so much of the American political spectrum for the cause. It backs the Vietnamese expedition with a coalition broad enough to include Republican Barry Goldwater, Democrat Lyndon Johnson, labor leader Meany, and John Roche of the ADA (thus reversing World War II's coalition, which excluded the far right and included the radical left). This bloc justifies the carnage in Vietnam with a huge image (carried over from old newsreels) of invading armies—making only one small change in the subtitle: the replacement of the word "Fascist" with the word "Communist." By this simple transplant, the whole savage arsenal of World War II—the means both justified and unjustifiable—supported by that great fund of indignation built against the Nazis, can be turned to fresh uses.

We should recall what happened at Munich: Chamberlain of England and Daladier of France met Hitler and Mussolini (this was September 30, 1938) and agreed to surrender the Sudeten part of Czechoslovakia, inhabited by German-speaking people, hoping thus to prevent a general war in Europe. Chamberlain returned to England, claiming he had brought "peace in our time." Six months later, Hitler had gobbled up the rest of Czechoslovakia; then he began presenting ultimatums to Poland; and by September 3, 1939, general war had broken out in Europe.

There is strong evidence that if the Sudetenland had not been surrendered at Munich—with it went Czechoslovakia's powerful fortifications, 70 percent of its iron, steel, and electric power, 86 percent of its chemicals, 66 percent of its coal—and that if Hitler had then gone to war, he would have been defeated quickly with the aid of Czechoslovakia's 35 well-trained divisions. And if he chose at the sign of resistance not to go to war, then at least, he would have been stopped in his expansion.

And so, the analogy continues, to let the Communist-dominated National Liberation Front win in South Vietnam is to encourage more Communist expansion in Southeast Asia and beyond, and perhaps lead to a war more disastrous than the present one; to stop Communism in South Vietnam is to discourage its expansion elsewhere.

We should note, first, some of the important differences between the Munich situation in 1938 and Vietnam today:

1. In 1938, the main force operating against the Czech *status quo* was an outside force, Hitler's Germany; the supporting force was the Sudeten group inside led by Konrad Henlein. Since 1958 (and traceable back to 1942), the major force operating

against the *status quo* in South Vietnam has been an inside force, formed in 1960 into the NLF; the chief supporter is not an outside nation but another part of the same nation, North Vietnam. The largest outside force in Vietnam consists of the American troops. To put it another way, in 1938, the Germans were trying to take over part of another country. Today, the Vietcong are trying to take over part of their own country. In 1938, the outsider was Germany. Today it is the United States.

2. The Czech government, whose interests the West surrendered to Hitler in 1938, was a strong, effective, prosperous, democratic government—the government of Benes and Masaryk. The South Vietnamese government which we support is a hollow shell of a government, unstable, unpopular, corrupt, a dictatorship of bullies and torturers, disdainful of free elections and representative government. They first opposed establishing a National Assembly on the ground that it might lead to Communism, and then held a totalitarian-type election controlled wholly by the government, headed by a long line of tyrants from Bao Dai to Diem to Ky, who no more deserve to be ranked with Benes and Masaryk than Governor Wallace of Alabama deserves to be compared to Albert Schweitzer. It is a government whose perpetuation is not worth the loss of a single human life.

3. Standing firm in 1938 meant engaging, in order to defeat once and for all, the central threat of that time, Hitler's Germany. Fighting in Vietnam today, even if it brings total victory, does not at all engage what the United States considers the central foes—the Soviet Union and Communist China. Even if international Communism *were* a single dangerous organism, to annihilate the Vietcong would be merely to remove a toenail from an elephant. To engage what the United States thinks is the source of its difficulties (Red China one day, Soviet Russia the next) would require nuclear war.

4. We have twenty years of cold-war history to test the proposition derived from the Munich analogy—that a firm stand in Vietnam is worth the huge loss of life, because it will persuade the Communists there must be no more uprisings elsewhere. But what effect did our refusal to allow the defeat of South Korea

(1950–53) or our aid in suppressing the Huk rebellion in the Philippines (1947–55) or the suppression of guerrillas in Malaya (1948–60) have on the guerrilla warfare in South Vietnam which started around 1958 and became consolidated under the National Liberation Front in 1960? If our use of subversion and arms to overthrow Guatemala in 1954 showed the Communists in Latin America that we meant business, then how did it happen that Castro rebelled and won in 1959? Did our invasion of Cuba in 1961, our blockade in 1962, show other revolutionaries in Latin America that they must desist? Then how explain the Dominican uprising in 1965? And did our dispatch of Marines to Santo Domingo end the fighting of guerrillas in the mountains of Peru?

One touches the Munich analogy and it falls apart.

The "domino theory" is another version of a similar idea. It was enunciated as early as April 7, 1954 by President Eisenhower at a press conference: "The loss of Indochina will cause the fall of Southeast Asia like a set of dominos." It was put in more sophisticated and scholarly form by Robert Scalapino (at the Washington Teach-In, 1965), who preferred to see it as a game of checkers, with China doing the jumping. (Others might call the game Monopoly and put the onus on the United States; my own temptation is to call the whole business Russian roulette.) Scalapino said:

> It seems to me clear that the arguments against American withdrawal are so powerful that they have not been answered, at least as yet. It is not merely that withdrawal would reduce American credibility with her allies and the neutrals around the world. It is also that a green light would be given to the new Communist-dominated National Liberation Movements even now getting underway. . . .
> American imperialism, asserts Peking, is a paper tiger. . . . American withdrawal from Viet-Nam would prove the Peking thesis correct, and make it virtually impossible for moderation to prevail within the Communist world. If the strategy of pushing America and forcing it into unilateral retreat works in Viet-Nam, it will work elsewhere and be tried everywhere.

. . . Peking . . . will move to those areas where she can com-
bine the ingredients necessary for her revolutionary formula.

Scalapino puts the burden of proof on the advocates of withdrawal ("the arguments . . . have not been answered"); it is
a curious reversal of the rules of evidence in civilized jurispru-
dence to say that someone under attack must present proof to
show why the attacker must stop! Surely, it is the other way
around. Not only must the United States prove why it must continue its ferocious assault on Vietnam, but the scale of violence
demands that it prove this beyond a reasonable doubt. We demand unanimity among twelve citizens before we will condemn
a single person to death, but we will destroy thousands of people
on a supposition as fragile as Eisenhower's dominos or Scalapino's checkers.

There is a good reason why the "domino theory" is the last
line of defense for the Vietnam hawks, and why they put the
burden of *disproving* it on their critics, while the bombs continue to fall. This is because the domino theory rests on supposi-
tions about the future, which are impossible to prove *con-
clusively* one way or the other. It is like saying: I will not stop
shooting at the fellow next door and his family until you can
assure me that he does not plan to burn my house down. No one
can say with any high degree of certainty *what* will happen if
Vietnam goes Communist, or what will happen if the Vietcong
are totally destroyed.

It is hard enough to say what will happen in Vietnam; but to
say that certain consequences in Asia, Africa, and Latin America
are inevitable, is absurd. International affairs are complex, and
predictions are extremely unreliable. Who would have predicted
the Tito break with Stalin, or destalinization in the Soviet Union,
or the Sino-Soviet split, or a Cuban socialist state, or the quick
overthrow of Nkrumah in Ghana and Sukarno in Indonesia, or
the American-Soviet detente, or a dozen other major events? To
be willing to commit huge numbers of people to death on a supposition about the future of world affairs is an incredible arrogance and a cruelty beyond words. It also means we have taken

over that doctrine which once horrified the humane liberals of this country: the doctrine of *preventive war*.

However, such a feat of prognostication becomes credible if we can locate one central body with both the power and the desire to execute a predicted series of evil acts. Scholars sometimes refer to this as the "devil theory" of history. Such a theory is simple, and inclusive, and is capable of mobilizing enormous fanaticism to the service of retribution. The "infidels" spurred the Crusades, "witches" brought the burnings and hangings of the Middle Ages, the Jews sent Germany into frenzies. In each case the accused were held responsible for all that was wrong, and their extinction was to bring glory and peace. In each case there could be no faltering; the hangman and machine-gun squad could not wait, because at the slightest sign of weakness the flood would engulf all.

Richard Hofstadter, in *The Paranoid Style in American Politics,* writes of "the central preconception of the paranoid style —the existence of a vast, insidious, preternaturally effective international conspiratorial network designed to perpetrate acts of the most fiendish character." Not long ago, the center of the conspiracy was Russia. Today, the devil is Communist China. A political scientist doing strategic research for the government told me one day in 1965, with complete calm, that his institute had decided they were completely wrong about the premise which underlay much of American policy in the postwar period —the premise that Russia hoped to take over Western Europe by force. Do we have any more evidence now to support our predictions about China than we had then about Russia?

Paranoia starts from a base of facts, but then leaps wildly to a conclusion. It is a fact that China is totalitarian in its limitation of free expression and fierce in its verbal assaults on the United States, that it crushed opposition in Tibet and fought for a strip of disputed territory on the Indian border. But again we are looking at a set of data in isolation.

Let's consider *India* briefly: It crushed an uprising in Hyderabad, initiated attacks on the China border, took Goa by force, and is fanatical in its insistence on Kashmir.

Are the Chinese behaving any more aggressively than most new nations (or old nations with new social systems)? They are, in fact, behaving *less* aggressively than did the United States in its early years, when it forced its way into Florida, made war with Mexico, even threatened Canada. Recall, too, the powerful concern of all new nations with security from attack: The United States after the Revolutionary War felt continually threatened by British outposts on its northwest frontiers and by the British Navy in the Atlantic; the resulting tension had a great deal to do with the War of 1812. Most scholarly observers of Communist China's behavior agree that its actions are *defensive* and that its talk about the atomic bomb being a "paper tiger" is not at all a threat, but an exclamation of defiance against the possibility that China would be attacked by American atomic power.

Take the following UPI dispatch of May 12, 1966: "Administration officials acknowledged Wednesday that the United States had rejected a Communist Chinese bid for an exchange of pledges that neither would be the first to use nuclear weapons against the other." How should the Chinese interpret that? How should they interpret this headline in *The New York Times* of October 23, 1964? "Washington Bars Any New Parley with China's Reds. Terms Peking's Suggestion for Nuclear Conference a 'Sucker' Proposal."

Is it not significant that China, which moved into North Korea when United States troops during the war approached its border, pulled its soldiers completely out of Korea after the truce was signed, unlike the United States? Or that China engaged Indian troops in the Himalayas only after being attacked in 1962, pushed the Indians almost to the plains of Assam, and then, with overwhelming power and a clear road ahead, declared a unilateral cease-fire and withdrew to what they had said was the correct boundary? How does one reconcile China's tolerance of the British nonmilitary control of a Chinese city (Hong Kong), and Portuguese control of another Chinese city (Macao) and their peaceful settlement of border problems with Pakistan, Burma, Nepal, Mongolia, with their fierce reaction to the Chiang-United States base on Taiwan? Does this not suggest

that their chief concern is the perennial concern of new nations
—physical security? And that they react with either ferocity or
tolerance depending on whether a nation is threatening this
security?

China, which is buffered by mountains and deserts on the
west, traditionally made contact with the rest of the world via
the Pacific Ocean. In mid-1966, China, on its Pacific side, faced
a sweeping arc of enormous American military power from
north to south: 40,000 troops in Japan; 60,000 in Korea; 50,000
on Guam and Okinawa; 50,000 on Formosa; 40,000 in the Philip-
pines; 25,000 in Thailand; 50,000 in the Seventh Fleet; 300,000
in South Vietnam.

In early 1954, Walter S. Robertson, the Assistant Secretary of
State for Far Eastern Affairs, testified to a House Appropriations
Committee on United States policy toward China, and his testimony was summarized by a member of the committee, with Robertson's approval, as follows:

> The heart of the present policy toward China and Formosa
> is that there is to be kept alive a constant threat of military
> action vis-à-vis Red China in the hope that at some point there
> will be an internal breakdown. . . . In other words, a cold
> war waged under the leadership of the U.S., with constant
> threat of attack against Red China, led by Formosa and other
> Far Eastern groups and militarily supported by the United
> States.

The United States has never repudiated that idea, and while it
does not repeat it publicly, its actions speak quite clearly to the
Chinese.

Certainly other Asian non-Communist countries should be
concerned about the "threat" of Communist China if it is real.
And while there is the normal concern of any small nation lest
any neighboring large nation encroach on its independence,
there is nothing like our hysteria (except for those like Chiang
Kai-shek, whose regimes are kept alive by our money and arms).
In early 1966, Alec Campbell, editor of *The New Republic* (a
magazine sympathetic to the Johnson administration until the

Vietnam escalation), toured the Far East. Hubert Humphrey had said on March 3, 1966, that "most Asian leaders are concerned about the belligerence and militancy of Communist China's attitudes." Campbell said in response, "I can find little evidence of their concern." He summed up his findings:

> Most Asians would like to see this country use its superior strength to quiet Chinese fears, not aggravate them; be big enough to overlook China's bad Communist habit of cursing and swearing; and seek through patience and courtesy an understanding with China such as we now seem to have reached with Russia.

As for our European allies, C. P. Fitzgerald, the English sinologist, puts it tersely in his book *Revolution in China.* "In fact, the Europeans accept the Chinese revolution as final, the Americans do not."

The American public at large has not followed the details of Chinese and United States policy in Asia in the past twenty years. It does read the headlines in the newspapers which keep pointing out that the Chinese *say* they are going to take over the world. But do they? Or is it another of these cases where eager reporters and politicians have substituted their own simple theory for one too elusive to be newsworthy?

Marxist theory itself gives no support to the notion of building a Communist world through outside aggression. With Marx, the internal contradictions of the capitalist system within each country would lead to social change; with Lenin, the especially sharp contradictions of world imperialism would bring uprisings in the colonial areas of the world; Stalin in *Economic Problems of Socialism in the USSR* (written at the end of World War II) continued to stress that the contradictions of imperialism would bring change. George Kennan has written:

> Central to the Soviet view of how socialism was to triumph on a world scale has always been the operation of social and political forces within the capitalist countries . . . it has never regarded action by its own forces as the main agency for the spread of world revolution. . . . In the course of the last

twenty years, I have labored many hours to explain to other Americans the nature of the Soviet threat as I saw it; in no respect have I found it so difficult to obtain understanding as in the presentation of this one simple fact.

Communist China, through all of her ideological disputation with the Soviet Union, has never departed from the idea that she agreed to in the Moscow Declaration of 1960, that Socialism "cannot be imposed from without."

There is, of course, Lin Piao's famous statement "Long Live the Victory of the People's War," written in 1965, which suffered the natural history of important documents: distortion in the mass media reaching millions, correction in the scholarly journals reaching thousands. What was held up before the public as a "blueprint of world conquest" turned out on closer inspection to be the usual Communist prediction that one day the world would be Communist, coupled with an exhortation to "Adhere to the Policy of Self-Reliance." The Chinese, Lin pointed out, had conducted their revolution "without any material aid from outside," and while people of the world should support one another against imperialism, "foreign aid can only play a supplementary role." Lin wrote:

> In order to make a revolution and to fight a people's war and be victorious, it is imperative to adhere to the policy of self-reliance, rely on the strength of the masses in one's own country and prepare to carry on the fight independently even when all material aid from outside is cut off.

American policy in Asia seems to be based, first, on distortions of what the Chinese say they want to do, and then on the supposition that they are omnipotent to do what we claim they want to do. In an article published in *Commentary* (April 1966), the Harvard expert on Asian politics, Benjamin Schwartz, brilliantly dissected this American "expectation that the whole third world is about to behave in a manner corresponding to Peking's optimum hopes for the future." Schwartz pointed to the strong nationalism in the underdeveloped world, as well as in the Communist world, to the craving everywhere for independence; he said the heterogeneity of the developing areas is not sufficiently understood by our policy-makers, and he concluded that the future of the third world "will continue to depend on local conditions within that world and not merely on the 'demonstration' effect of Vietnam."

To say (as Scalapino did) that "American withdrawal from Vietnam would prove the Peking thesis correct" is to misunderstand the "Peking thesis," which has repeatedly said that while in the long run the United States is a paper tiger, it could be a *genuine* tiger in the short run. Thus, American victory in Vietnam would not disprove the thesis, any more than the failure of the Philippine rebellion in the 1950s disproved it. Scalapino underestimates the power of Marxist ideology, which will go on asserting the need for revolutions no matter how many times and in how many places they are crushed.

To then say, "If the strategy of pushing America and forcing it into unilateral retreat works in Vietnam, it will work elsewhere," is to assume some devilish strategist behind the upheavals taking place all over the world. Can we rest so heavy a moral burden as our indiscriminate bombing in Vietnam on the weak proposition that victory there will *stop* revolutionary movements elsewhere, or that withdrawal from Vietnam will *produce* revolutions elsewhere? The presumably "hard-headed" realists turn out to be the foggiest romanticists.

The history of the birth of Communist states does not support the idea that such revolutions come about as the result of some central strategy, conceived by an outside power. Both of the giant revolutions—in Russia and China—were the result of indigenous conditions. The Cuban revolution certainly was not masterminded from outside. In Eastern Europe, the Red Army was in the area, having pushed Hitler's army back to the Elbe, but it did not initiate the social revolutions in this region; rather, it played a supporting role for upheavals that came about primarily as a reaction against Nazi occupation, and against prewar governments which were either semifeudal or semi-Fascist. The war shattered rotten social structures, with powerful local Communist movements coming out of the ruins.

Paul Zinner's paper for the American Historical Association (*Communist Seizures of Power: Czechoslovakia*) emphasizes the powerful indigenous support for Communism and the popularity of the Communist Party in Czechoslovakia, enabling a peaceful seizure of power in 1948, with no Red Army troops in the country and with "no certainty that Russian troops would have moved across the border." Thus revolution was fundamentally an internal matter, though the nearby presence of the Soviet Union constituted psychological support. Even stronger evidence comes from the Yugoslav situation, where the Red Army played no role at all, but where Communism developed out of internal conditions similar to those in the other countries of Eastern Europe.

If Communism is not in most cases imposed from without, then perhaps one must still thwart the creation of a Communist state in Vietnam because it will be an *example* for others. But do revolutionaries anywhere really need *another* example? There have been two huge ones in the world for some time, and a dozen smaller ones. If Castro can subsist off the American shore, then no matter what happens in Vietnam, or five Vietnams, need any revolutionary movement surrender hope? And besides, do revolutionaries *ever* give up, if their passion against the regime keeps being fed by its abuses? We often reveal the customary arrogance of the power-holder who cannot understand the determination, the perseverance, the spirit of self-sacrifice, of the revolutionary.

The *closest* dominos to Vietnam are Laos, Cambodia, Thailand, and Burma. Of these, the countries that are most secure and most independent are, curiously, those countries where there has been no American military intervention, which are unprotected by United States military forces, which have friendly relations with Communist China—Burma and Cambodia. Burma has a 1000-mile border with Communist China, longer than her border with Laos and Thailand, and if she has not been knocked over into Communism by that huge domino to her north, why should it happen even if Laos and Thailand were Communist? General Gavin told the Foreign Relations Commit-

tee (February 8, 1966) that Thailand, a military autocracy cov-
ered with United States air bases, would have difficulties with
guerrillas *whatever* happened in Vietnam.

It seems to be precisely the countries most heavily dependent
on United States military aid that are the most unstable. This is
not just an ironic accident but contains an internal logic. Once
you discard the notion that Communist revolutions will be
master-minded from Peking or, if not that, will spread by example or subversion from one place to the next, then you return
from devil-theory and magic to history. After all, we *do* have a
history of fourteen countries that turned Communist, and what
we find in their history is one or both of two factors: (1) intolerable socio-economic conditions, (2) a vacuum created by the
devastation of war. This suggests that to bring war or near-war
conditions into a country that already has serious internal problems is the most effective way to break whatever thin threads
hold such a society together. A military solution for the problems
of underdeveloped countries, in other words, becomes self-
defeating, tending to bring about exactly what it is supposed to
prevent.

Much of the discussion on Vietnam has centered on the question of whether we can "win" in Vietnam. A more pertinent
question is whether we *should* win, in the sense of a military
victory. "Victory" for the United States in the cold war has too
often meant the maintenance of a repressive oligarchy in power,
ignoring the needs of the population, and holding on by its teeth
to a brass ring held by an American general.

Korea is one example. There we "won" in the sense that we
prevented the North Koreans from forcibly unifying the country. But the cost of Korea in human terms was frightful. General
O'Donnell, head of the Bomber Command in the Far East: "I
would say that the entire, almost the entire Korean peninsula is
just a terrible mess. Everything is destroyed. There is nothing
standing worthy of the name." Napalm was poured onto villages.
(*Time* magazine, counting South Korea's losses after the war—
400,000 civilians killed, 100,000 children made orphans—added
this characteristic sentence: "But out of disaster has grown a

tough army of 16 divisions, and a sense of manhood.") And what was the result? A series of *junta* dictatorships, the end of political democracy, 25 percent unemployment in 1960, and 40 percent of the farm families with less than an acre of land.

The tragic story was summed up in 1961 by Harvard's expert on Korea, Edward W. Wagner ("Failure in Korea," *Foreign Affairs,* October 1961), who noted that 70,000 Korean residents in Japan chose repatriation to North Korea where a Communist government, with serious deficiencies in political freedom, was nevertheless making rapid economic progress, improving the general standard of living, and so offered "the better hope for the future."

What did the Korean nightmare of horrors accomplish? It "showed the Communists," as politicians and others kept repeating, that "we mean business." But six years later, revolutionaries under Castro took over in Cuba. Seven years later, the National Liberation Front was formed in Vietnam, and today 40,000 Koreans are fighting *there.*

Two premises of the domino theory deserve to be reexamined. One is that we should be concerned about the maintenance of American military bases near Vietnam, in Southeast Asia, and in the Pacific area in general. The United States armed forces do not really "protect" any nation; only a nation whose stability and strength come from its own resources can really maintain its independence, and the presence of foreign forces undermines that stability and saps that strength.

We ought to say firmly what many Americans, even those disturbed by the Vietnam war, have been too timorous to say, that American military forces do not belong in Southeast Asia or anywhere in Asia at all (indeed, that *no* nation in the world should have troops or bases anywhere outside its borders). Are such bases necessary to "national security"? Again, we have become victims of a phrase repeated so often that it becomes unquestioned. Are we to seriously believe that China—or anybody—will attack the United States? Our bases in Asia do nothing to protect America. But they do keep unpopular regimes in power; they threaten China and thus perpetuate hostility between two huge nations which have no reason to be in conflict with one another.

The other unexamined premise in the domino theory is that it is necessarily bad for revolutions to take place in other parts of Asia. If a victory for Communism in Vietnam is followed by upheavals in other Asian countries where conditions demand change, why should we object? And why should we assume that these upheavals will be the result of the "domino" effect rather than of the strivings for betterment that people have shown everywhere since human society was formed? We seem unable to believe that hunger, homelessness, oppression are sufficient spurs to revolution, without plotting from the outside.

So Communism and revolution require discussion. They are basic to that inversion of morality which enables the United States to surround the dirty war in Vietnam with the righteous glow of the war against Hitler.

A key assumption in this inversion is that Communism and Nazism are sufficiently identical to be treated alike. However, Communism as a set of ideals has attracted good people—not racists, or bullies, or militarists—all over the world. One may argue that in Communist countries citizens had better affirm their allegiance to it, but that doesn't account for the fact that millions in France, Italy, and Indonesia have been Communist party members, that countless others all over the world have been inspired by Marxian ideals. And why should they not? These ideals include peace, brotherhood, racial equality, the classless society, the withering away of the state.

True, the Communists behave much better out of power than in it. However, that is a commentary not on their ideals but on weaknesses which they share with non-Communist wielders of power. If, presumably in pursuit of their ideals, they have resorted to brutal tactics, maintained suffocating bureaucracies and rigid dogmas, that makes them about as reprehensible as other nations, other social systems, which—while boasting of the Judeo-Christian heritage—have fostered war, exploitation, colonialism, and race hatred. We judge ourselves by our ideals, others by their actions. It is a great convenience.

The ultimate values of the Nazis, let us recall, included racism, elitism, militarism, and war as ends in themselves. Unlike either the Communist nations or the capitalist democracies, there is here no ground for appeal to higher purposes. The ideological basis for coexistence between Communist and capitalist nations is the rough consensus of ultimate goals which they share. While war is held off, the citizens on both sides—and this is beginning to occur—will increasingly insist that their leaders live up to these values.

One of these professed values—which the United States is trying with difficulty to conceal by fragile arguments and feeble analogies—is the self-determination of peoples. Self-determination justifies the overthrow of entrenched oligarchies, whether foreign or domestic, in ways that will not lead to general war. China, Egypt, Indonesia, Algeria, and Cuba are examples. Such revolutions tend to set up dictatorships, but they do so in the name of values which can be used to erode those same dictatorships. They therefore deserve as much general support and specific criticism as did the American revolutionaries, who set up a pro-slavery government—but with a commitment to freedom which later led the nation *against its wishes,* to abolitionism.

The easy use of the term "totalitarian" to cover both Nazis and Communists, or to equate the South Vietnamese regime with that of Ho Chi Minh, fails to make important distinctions, just as dogmatists of the left sometimes fail to distinguish between Fascist states and capitalist democracies.

This is ahistorical on two counts. First, it ignores the fact that, for the swift economic progress needed by new nations today, a Communist-led regime does an effective job (though it is not the only type of new government that can). In doing so, it raises educational and living standards, and thus paves the way (as the USSR and Eastern Europe already show) for attacks from within on its own thought-control system. Second, one forgets that the United States and Western Europe, now haughty in prosperity, with a fair degree of free expression, built their present status on the backs of either slaves or colonial people,

and subjected their own laboring populations to several generations of misery before beginning to look like welfare states.

The perspective of history suggests that a united Vietnam under Ho Chi Minh is preferable to the elitist dictatorship of the
South, just as Maoist China with all its faults is preferable to
the rule of Chiang, and Castro's Cuba to Batista's. We do not
have pure choices in the present, although we should never
surrender those values which can shape the future. Right now, for
Vietnam, a Communist government is probably the best avenue
available to that whole packet of human values which make up
the common morality of mankind today; the preservation of human life, self-determination, economic security, the end of race
and class oppression, and that freedom of speech and press which
an educated population begins to demand.

In the debate on Vietnam, there has been little or no discussion on exactly what would be the evil consequences of a united
Communist Vietnam. It has become an article of faith that what
is good or bad in international relations is a matter of counting
up the countries that are on the Communist side, and the number that are on our side. There is the black eye, and there is the
feather in the cap. And the difference is worth a mountain of
corpses.

We need to get accustomed to the idea that there will be more
Communist countries in the world, and that this is not necessarily bad. The physical security of the United States is not
diminished by that fact in itself; Communist nations in their
international affairs behave very much like other nations (this
is why they are so often disappointing to their sympathizers);
some are friendly, some are hostile. Each is a unique resultant
of Marxist theory and local conditions. The more there are, the
greater diversity there will be among them. It is several years
now since scholars in the field of Communist studies began taking note of "polycentrism," but American officials still often
act as if there were one Communist center in the world.

One thing we should have learned by now is that Communist
nations are as prone to the emotion of nationalism as other na-

tions; they crave independence and resist domination by *any* other nation, whether capitalist or Communist. What this means is that a small but effective Communist nation which is neighbor to a large one can guard its independence far better than a non-Communist, semifeudal dictatorship. A Communist Vietnam under Ho Chi Minh can be expected to retain its independence as surely as Tito has maintained his.

The idea of "containment" has always been ambiguous: Is it our aim to contain China, or to contain Communism? And if it is *both*, then what do we do if the two aims turn out to be in conflict with one another?

To base our entire Asian policy on "containing" China is to risk billions of dollars and thousands of lives on the idea that China plans to take over other countries by military expansion —a hypothesis not supported either by her words or by the history of her behavior so far, and one that in the case of the Soviet Union turned out to be false. And to make the hypothesis doubly faulty, it assumes that even if China *wanted* to expand, she could.

But what if China, though not bent on military expansion, is tempted (like all great powers, dictatorial or democratic) to establish undue influence over some neighboring country simply because a power vacuum has been created there by a weak and unstable regime? If so, would not the most effective deterrent to this be the existence of a relatively strong and stable *Communist* regime in that country? Which is more able to stand on its own feet, to feel secure—the right-wing dictatorship of South Korea, which requires 60,000 United States troops to buttress the government, or the Communist welfare dictatorship of North Korea? In mid-August 1966, North Korea, which has a long border with China and a short border with the Soviet Union, declared her independence of both of them, saying it was "impermissible" for a big Communist party to impose its will on a small one, and that underdeveloped countries must build up an independent national economy or they would be "unable to defend their political independence."

To extend this to Vietnam, would not the purposes both of

stability in Asia and the independence of Vietnam be best served by a Communist Vietnam on the border of China? Richard Lowenthal of the Free University of Berlin, the author of *World Communism,* wrote (November 21, 1965) in *The New York Times*:

> In Moscow's view, the Communists are the only solid politi-cal force in Vietnam; hence the only hope of limiting Chinese influence in the Indochinese peninsula lies in giving the local Communists a chance to unify the country without prolonging the war, ending their one-sided dependence on Chinese sup-port. I must admit that, in this case, the Soviet analysis seems to me more realistic than the American. . . .

We will probably be safer in a world sprinkled with the likes of Ho Chi Minh, Kim Il Sung, and Tito, than with Chiang, Park, and Ky.

We should keep in mind that, at this point in history, Com-munism is only part of a much broader movement—the rising of hungry and harassed people in Asia, Africa, Latin America (and parts of the United States). Forgetting this, we try to crush insurrection in one place (Greece, Iran, Guatemala, the Philip-pines, etc.) and apparently succeed, only to find a revolution—whether Communist or Socialist or nationalist or of indescrib-able character—springing up somewhere else. We surround the world with our navy, cover the sky with our planes, fling our money to the winds, and then a revolution takes place in Cuba, nearby. (If Harlem Negroes tried to take over Manhattan, would we blame that on Castro?) We see every rebellion as the result of some plot concocted in Moscow or Peking, when what is really happening is that people everywhere want to eat and to be free and will use desperate means, and any one of a number of social systems, to achieve their ends.

The other side makes the same mistake. The Russians face a revolt in Hungary or Poznan and attribute it to bourgeois in-fluence or to American scheming. But the problem is not that China or America want to take over the world. (Maybe they do, but they can't.) The problem is, rather, that various peoples want to take over their parts of the world, and without the courtesies that attend normal business transactions.

We want stability in the world. But a stability based on starvation or on the rule of landlords and generals is not worth saving. Neither is it really stable. Revolutions are going to take place, whether we like it or not. Their aim, no matter how zigzag their path, is somehow to achieve the very values that all major countries, East and West, *claim* to uphold: self-determination, economic security, racial equality, freedom. We ought to clear that path, not blow it up.

A Communist Vietnam, if popularly based, is as much a part of this revolution as a non-Communist Egypt, or a Kenya which talks of "African Socialism." The withdrawal of the United States, by leaving the field open to the play of forces which are *Vietnamese,* will probably leave the National Liberation Front, which is Communist-dominated and already administers about one-third of South Vietnam, to become the chief force in a new South Vietnamese government; eventually there would be a unified Communist North Vietnam.

A large part of South Vietnam, judging from the size and the morale of the guerrilla forces and from the reports of anti-Communists like Robert Scigliano, is pro-Communist. (Scigliano writes: "The fact is that Communism in the dress of nationalism and in its advocacy of land to the peasants, represents a powerful force in South Vietnam, and one which receives widespread support from the peasant population.") American correspondents consistently report that another large part of Vietnam—under government control—seems to want peace first of all, regardless of the form of government they live under. Very few —and the size of the American forces there attest to this—want to fight for the regime we support. Surely the United States has no right to decide for 12,000,000 men, women, and children that they are better off dead than Red. It should, therefore, remove its human and mechanical instruments of death from Vietnam.

But can we just . . . withdraw?

9. Withdrawal

SENATOR HICKENLOOPER of Iowa was questioning George Kennan at the Senate Foreign Relations Committee Hearings in early 1966:

> Hickenlooper: Now, there are problems facing us and others. . . . How we disengage ourselves without losing a tremendous amount of face or position in various areas of the world.
>
> Kennan: Senator, I think precisely the question, the consideration that you have just raised is the central one that we have to think about; and it seems to me, as I have said here, that a precipitate, sudden, and unilateral withdrawal would not be warranted by circumstances now.

A bit later in the questioning:

> Hickenlooper: Do you think the rather immediate withdrawal of the United States forces and our activity in South Vietnam from that country could be used effectively as a propaganda tool and weapon in Africa and in the emerging nations of Africa?
>
> Kennan: Senator, it would be a six months' sensation, but I dare say we would survive it in the end, and there would be another day. Things happen awfully fast on the international scene, and people's memories are very short. . . .

Kennan's testimony on the matter of withdrawal is important because it is representative of a large body of influential opinion which says flatly we must not withdraw, but then cannot really give persuasive reasons why we should not. Prestige, Kennan says, is the "central question" if we withdraw, but then he adds that it would be a "six months' sensation" and "we would survive it in the end."

In *Triumph or Tragedy,* Richard Goodwin argues that withdrawal "would damage the confidence of all Asian nations, and of many other nations, in the willingness and the ability of the United States to protect them against attack." But it seems that most Asians and "many other nations" disagree completely with Goodwin; they would like us to leave Vietnam. And one can readily see why: We are "protecting" Vietnam by killing its people and destroying its land. Who else would want such protection?

Toward the end of his book, Goodwin makes an odd statement. He says: "In the South we have no choice but to continue the war. We are under attack and withdrawal is impossible and unwise." Are we not "under attack" because we are *there,* and is it not true that if we withdrew we would no longer be under attack?

General Gavin, who preceded Kennan as a major witness before the Fulbright Committee, had an exchange with Senator Frank Church of Idaho:

> Church: Now, if we had not intervened in the interim since . . . and if we had not made the pledges that have been made to the Saigon government, and committed American presence and prestige there; in other words, if you were again faced with the same question . . . would you still be of the same opinion that the vital security interests of the United States from a military standpoint do not require the deployment of American troops in Indochina?
>
> Gavin: Yes, sir. I would say so. "Vital" is the key word there.

It turns out that a remarkable number of high-placed officials agree that the United States should never have become involved in military intervention in Vietnam. But now that she has done so, they feel an important matter of "prestige" is involved. For instance, in a roundup of opinion in the Senate which *New York Times* reporter E. W. Kenworthy made in the summer of 1965, he found that "many of these silent Senators" told reporters off-the-record that they wished the United States "had never gone into Vietnam; they would like to get out, even at the cost of a political compromise amounting to defeat, but they will not advocate military withdrawal under fire."

We are dealing here with an odd logic: that it was wrong for the United States to get involved in the first place, because Vietnam is simply not "vital" for American security, but that we must not withdraw from a move that was both wrong and costly because now our "prestige" is involved. This must mean that the stake in prestige is enormously important. It was so important to Senator Frank Church that when Gavin said he *still* felt no vital United States interests were at stake, Church immediately said:

> I wanted to get that on the record, General, because there has been so much discussion of withdrawal, and I do not know anyone around this table, certainly no member of the Foreign Relations Committee, that has advocated a withdrawal . . . under the present circumstances . . . in Vietnam. But . . . we have made a very great commitment of American prestige and a very solemn political commitment that has to be thrown into the balance. . . .

Not one member of the Senate Foreign Relations Committee would advocate withdrawal, even those as critical of United States policy as Fulbright, Morse, Church, Gore, and Clark. The "solemn political commitment" to General Ky could hardly be considered more solemn than the nation's commitment to the Geneva Accords, to the United Nations Charter, to the Constitution of the United States, all of which have been ignored by United States policy in Vietnam. What is left is "prestige," and it must be that even for the Senators criticizing the administration this weighed so heavily in "the balance" Church spoke of that none would call for withdrawal. The factor of "prestige" would then have to outweigh all else that stemmed from the admitted original error of engagement in Vietnam: billions of dollars, thousands of lives, and also, untold dollars, lives, and dangers in the future. To balance all *that* the prestige factor would need to be of overwhelming significance. Let us see.

Kennan himself, in his testimony, talked about "the damage being done to the feelings entertained for us by the Japanese people" by the present policy and said "the confidence and good disposition of the Japanese is the greatest asset we have had and the greatest asset we could have in East Asia." Does not the loss of United States prestige in Japan—"the greatest asset . . . in East Asia" rank at least equal to the "six months' sensation" that Kennan said would be the cost of our withdrawal? And if to Japan we add England, France, indeed, most of Western Europe, as well as Africa and Latin America, where our prestige has suffered badly as a result of the Vietnam policy, does it not seem likely that the result of withdrawal would be a net *gain* in prestige?

History does not show that a nation which liquidates a bad venture suffers a serious loss of prestige where it can compensate in other ways. Proud, powerful England surrendered to the ragtag thirteen American colonies, removed her armed forces ignominiously, and did not suffer for it. More recently, and more pertinently, France moved out voluntarily from Algeria and from Indochina; today she has more prestige than ever before. The Soviet Union pulled her missiles out of Cuba; her prestige has not suffered, and many people who feared World War III was coming feel a certain gratitude for her prudence. Hans Morgenthau, who has spent a good part of his scholarly career analyzing international relations and who made his reputation as a hard-headed "realist," not as an "idealist," has written:

> Is it really a boon to the prestige of the most powerful nation on earth to be bogged down in a war which it is neither able to win nor can afford to lose? This is the real issue which is presented by the argument of prestige.

So far I have been talking only about prestige as a flat, one-dimensional quantity. But more important is its *quality*. There is a kind of prestige this nation should not worry about losing —that which is attached to sheer power, to victory by force of arms, devoid of moral content. Which is more terrible: to have people in the world say that the United States withdrew from an untenable situation, or to have it said, as is now being said everywhere, that the United States is acting foolishly and immorally in Vietnam?

For George Kennan, there is no vital reason for the United
States to stay in Vietnam, even knowing its withdrawal would
probably lead to a Communist-dominated Vietnam, *except* for
prestige. As he told the Committee:

> If it were not for the considerations of prestige that arise
> precisely out of our present involvement, even a situation in
> which South Vietnam was controlled exclusively by the Viet-
> cong, while regrettable and no doubt morally unwarranted,
> would not, in my opinion, present dangers great enough to
> justify our direct military intervention.

And if, upon examination, this "prestige" turns out to be empty
(using Kennan's own example of Japan, plus what else we
know), there is hardly anything left to support our "direct military intervention."

Then why, instead of simply urging immediate withdrawal,
do Kennan, Gavin, and Morgenthau advance the "enclave" theory: that United States forces should stop bombing and retire to
a few strong positions on the coast? All of them, not believing
that a United States presence in Vietnam is vital, are really suggesting this as a half-way step to withdrawal. The presumption
is that holding on to enclaves would also hold on to a bit of prestige, and unlike "precipitate, sudden, unilateral" withdrawal,
would give us time to negotiate our way out of Vietnam.

This proposal, however, comes too late in the history of the
conflict in Vietnam. By now, the war against the Vietcong is
mainly an American war; by September 1966, United States
forces were larger than the regular forces of the Ky government.
With American bombings ended and troops withdrawn, the Saigon government would collapse. Would it serve American "prestige" to stand by in enclaves while the Ky government fell apart
to be replaced by a government which—whether Buddhist-
neutralist or Vietcong—would ask or tell the United States to
leave?

It would be far less ignominious for the United States to decide
to leave on its own—before it is asked by a new government in
South Vietnam. Speedy withdrawal need not be shameful; this

is not a Dunkirk situation where decimated troops, harassed on ground and air, scramble into boats and flee. The United States controls the air, the ports, the sea; it can make the most graceful, the most magestic withdrawal in history. Of course it could not do this in a day or a week; it would need to pull its troops from the interior to the coast (so that *temporarily* there would be something like "enclaves"), and then transport them away from Vietnam as quickly as ships and planes can carry them.

The enclave proposal comes too late in another sense. The supposition is that United States troops could be concentrated in enclaves while negotiations proceeded, at the end of which they would come home. But what would be the point of this? At one time, it might have been argued that this would create the show-of-force on the spot which would enable the United States to negotiate from a position of some strength. But this implies there is something to negotiate *for*. If there once was, that time is past. Earlier in the war, the National Liberation Front might possibly have settled for some solution less than a dominant position in South Vietnam. For instance, right after Diem's assassination in November 1963 (according to *The New York Times* and the *Manchester Guardian,* and cited in the American Friends Service Committee's *Peace in Vietnam*), Hanoi was willing to discuss a coalition, neutralist government in South Vietnam. But at that time Rusk turned down a French proposal for a neutral, independent South Vietnam, and the following July the United States rejected a suggestion by U Thant, accepted by France, the USSR, Peking, and Hanoi, to reconvene the Geneva Conference. On July 24, 1964, responding to De-Gaulle's plea to reconvene at Geneva, President Johnson told the press: "We do not believe in conferences called to ratify terror, so our policy is unchanged." (See Schurmann, *et al., The Politics of Escalation in Vietnam.*) By April 1965, the negotiating position of Hanoi had become hardened into four points which included settling Vietnam affairs "in accordance with the program of the National Liberation Front."

It is an old story in the history of rebellion. The American colonists would have been ready to accept some solution less than independence in early 1775, but by January 1776 they were committed to no less than independence. Negroes in Montgomery, Alabama were ready at one point in the 1955 campaign on bus desegregation to accept merely a modified form of desegregation; but by the time their movement had crystallized they would accept nothing less than total integration. Richard Goodwin points (in *Triumph or Tragedy*) to the increasing militancy of the other side, despite our ferocious bombing, and says:

> We cannot know the will of men we do not understand. From Thermopylae to the Japanese-infested islands of the Pacific and Hitler's Berlin bunker, history is full of individuals and fighting forces who chose to fight against impossible odds and accept certain death.

Goodwin points to the dilemma of negotiations *at this stage*: the Vietcong will not accept any settlement that does not give them "a role in the political life of the country"; and at the same time, "it is unlikely we will permit any government to come to power which would inflict on us what some would see as the 'humiliation' of requesting our withdrawal."

By now, the Vietcong (and their friends in the North) have sacrificed too much to settle for anything less than a South Vietnam in which the NLF plays the major role, and from which United States troops completely withdraw. And if this is the only possible successful outcome of negotiations with a determined revolutionary foe, what is the point of negotiating? It might be argued that such a settlement might be made in effect, but tied with enough pretty bows and frills to make it *look* as if the United States had gained something from it. The world will hardly be deceived; the deception will last a short time, and there will be a much longer time—no matter what we do—for other countries to contemplate the fact that the United States had, whatever the niceties, departed from Vietnam.

True, there are certain developments to be hoped for when the present government and its American military support are gone. But none of these—except one—depends on the presence of United States soldiers. That one positive thing which the United States can do, as it departs, is to take with it those government officials, army officers, and others who fear for their lives when a new government comes in. These people could be resettled in any of a dozen places. Are we required to stay in Vietnam, as some have suggested, in order to "meet our pledges" to the present officialdom, when this seems to require killing their fellow countrymen in large numbers in order to keep them alive? Surely our job is not to go around the world protecting semifeudal dictatorships from the wrath of revolutionaries. It is a historical fact that revolutionaries, after victory, are merciless with those of the old regime. After World War II, Frenchmen executed—without benefit of trial—thousands of former Nazi collaborators. (We might note that the United States government, which seems very concerned with what might happen to Vietnamese officials, was silent when 250,000 Indonesians, said to be Communists, were massacred.) With a bit of inconvenience, we can save many of those in Vietnam who are in danger.

The other desirable developments cannot be guaranteed, indeed can only be thwarted, by United States military presence. One of these is the establishment of a government in which not only the NLF, but Buddhist, Montagnard, and other elements play a role. This we will have to leave to the Buddhists and others to work for; they are quite militant and capable of pressing for their rights. The United States cannot negotiate, for any future component of government in South Vietnam, a strength which does not exist. If it does exist, then the Vietnamese must negotiate it for themselves. The presence of the United States can only distort the true balance of forces, and only a settlement which represents this balance can be stable.

What was fundamentally wrong with the Geneva Agreement was that the great powers dominated it and falsified the real relationship of forces. All the North and half the South were under Vietminh control, and the division of the country into two equal parts was bound to fail. Not only the United States, but also the Soviet Union and China, were responsible for this development, because their own national ambitions required a peaceful settlement, even at the expense of the Vietminh. Neither

Communism nor capitalism, it seems, can be depended on to look out for the interests of *other* nations.

We say we want economic well-being for Vietnam. But this, too, is more likely to be hurt than helped by our military occupation. We can be quite sure that an independent South Vietnam, first alone, and then in union with the North, will engage in the kind of economic experimentation and development that Communist countries in different parts of the world have done, and quite successfully. This is part of the modernization process that other, non-Communist nations of Asia and Africa are going through. It will be hard, progress will be uneven, and there will be sacrifices, unjustly distributed perhaps. But that is how it was in the West in its period of swift industrial growth.

What else would we presumably like to get out of staying and negotiating: political freedom? This is hard to come by in any part of the economically undeveloped world, whether Communist or non-Communist. We have not been very successful in developing this in those parts of the world dominated by the United States, though we fondly include them in "the free world." Vietnam will probably have to go through a long evolutionary struggle for this, as have most countries in the world, whether Communist or not.

There is a good deal of evidence to show that political liberty is related to economic security. As nations grow less desperate in the struggle for necessities, as education spreads, as young people speak out, society becomes more open; this has been happening in the Soviet Union and in Eastern Europe. This means that the best way we can show our concern for both the economic well-being and the political freedom of the Vietnamese is to take the billions that have gone for death and turn them to the service of life. We should offer several billions in economic aid to North and South Vietnam, with no strings attached; or, better still, we can put that money into a United Nations fund which will then go to Vietnam under international sponsorship.

A United States military presence is a danger to the Vietnamese and to us. Its withdrawal is neither "abdication of responsibility" nor "isolationism." Our bombing and shooting are irresponsible.

In the future, we can show our responsibility by giving economic aid, when invited. We can be isolationist in the military sense; we can be internationalist in the economic and cultural fields.

The United States, thus, cannot gain anything for Vietnam by negotiating, and it *should not gain anything for itself*. Since this country does not belong in Vietnam it has no moral basis for negotiating any status for itself—certainly not military bases or troops; Vietnam has had enough of that.

There is something intrinsically wrong in the idea that the United States should participate in negotiations to decide the future of Vietnam. We are an outside power, and the fact that we have inundated the country with combat soldiers does not thereby give us any moral right to decide its fate. Perhaps might makes right, as a historical fact, but it *should not* make right; and it is the duty of citizens to assert the "shoulds," however statesmen behave.

This is true also for China, the Soviet Union, England, and all other great powers. To have the future of Vietnam decided by these outside powers at an international conference is as much a violation of self-determination as was the settlement of Czechoslovakia's fate by Hitler, Mussolini, Daladier, and Chamberlain in 1938 at Munich. Whatever negotiation goes on should be among the Vietnamese themselves, each group negotiating from its own position of strength, undistorted by the strength of the great powers. This would give the present government virtually no voice in the future of the country, because it has—without United States backing—virtually no strength. It would give the Buddhist groups an important voice, because they represent significant numbers of people, whose support any future government must have. And it would undoubtedly give the National Liberation Front the major voice. (In September 1966, the NLF reasserted its willingness to work with other Vietnamese groups in a future government, and to desist from reprisals against former foes. This has been a basic part of its program, as Staughton Lynd and Tom Hayden point out in the book reporting their trip to Hanoi, *The Other Side*.)

In this light, to ask whether the United States will be willing to negotiate with the Vietcong seems strange. Rather, the question is: Should the Vietcong be willing to negotiate with the United States? From a standpoint of moral principle it should not; from the standpoint of military reality it may have to. But it is the oppressive power of *our* country which forces this violation of moral principle, and it is the duty of American citizens—whatever the reality of power—to try to bend the power of government toward what is *right*.

For the United States to withdraw unilaterally, leaving the negotiating to the various groups in Vietnam, would avoid the present impasse over negotiations. This impasse is founded on a set of psychological realities which protract the war. The National Liberation Front, imbued with the spirit of patriots driving off an invading army, is willing to continue its guerrilla tactics until the United States is worn down. Besides, the Geneva experience taught it to distrust international agreements; it is confident of its skill in the jungles of Vietnam, not so confident it can outmaneuver great powers at conference tables. The United States government appears divided in its intentions, between its spokesmen for peace (like Goldberg at the United Nations) and its military minds bent on victory. (The same day that Goldberg proposed peace talks at the United Nations—September 28, 1966—McNamara announced an increase in bomber production for Vietnam.)

To wait until all of the sensitive and stubborn elements are fitted together in that intricate mechanism of negotiation—the NLF, its sympathizers and advisers in Hanoi, the split personalities of the Johnson administration, plus its client government in Saigon—is to consign thousands more each month to injury or death. Does it really absolve us of guilt to say that "they" won't talk with us, and so we must continue killing? Does "their" stubbornness end *our* responsibility? No actor in this complex situation has more freedom to act, has less to lose by so acting, has greater resources to fall back on, than the United States. The sanity of unilateral withdrawal is that it makes the end of the war independent of anyone's consent but our own. It is clean-cut, it is swift, it is right.

Some say that the administration, even if it decided on such a move, could not do it, because it is not feasible "politically"; that is, the American public would not accept it. According to this argument, the "prestige" that everyone talks about our losing by withdrawal is really prestige at home.

But the argument is weak. The Johnson administration has *not* gained prestige from its Vietnam actions. The national polls show that the public has gradually, steadily lost faith in this administration. In September 1966, less than half of those polled throughout the country voiced support for the administration's Vietnam policy. It is true that the polls do not show a substantial number of Americans in favor of withdrawal. But it is also true that most Americans are tired of the war and wish we would get out, one way or another. Many think this is best done by military escalation; others by de-escalation; but the idea of *ending the war* is the most common feeling.

Withdrawal has not drawn large support, because it has not been put forward either by the administration or by its most prominent critics. And so the public has been forced to choose within a limited set of respectable alternatives. If the administration were to advance a new alternative, it would soon gain the respectability that *any* proposal gets which is made by the leaders of government.

In the 1966 elections, one American city—Dearborn, Michigan—confronted its citizens directly with the issue of withdrawal, by asking on the ballot: "Are you in favor of an immediate cease-fire and withdrawal of U.S. troops from Viet Nam so the Vietnamese people can settle their own problems?" Of those voting (34,791) 41 percent voted for withdrawal. The issue had been put on the ballot by the Mayor, an ex-Marine, who said: "I think the war is illegal. If I were a young fellow, I certainly wouldn't go to Viet Nam. I'd rather spend three years on a rock pile than to fight some poor little barefoot guys who have never done anything to us."

What is remarkable, it seems to me, is that in spite of a

barrage of arguments from the nation's leaders *against* withdrawal, with no one high in government and no one in the national mass media arguing for withdrawal, 41 percent of the citizens of Dearborn (a rather conservative city, traditionally) should vote for such a solution. What might the result have been if, for just one week, national political leaders and the press had been giving the arguments *for* withdrawal?

It may be sad to note, but the American public (and probably, *any* public anywhere) is extremely changeable and open to suggestion, especially when the suggestion comes from on high. When Woodrow Wilson said the United States was too proud to fight in World War I, the public went along. When he then said the United States must fight in World War I, the public again went along. FDR said he would keep the nation out of war and was reelected. He took aggressive steps toward the Axis and we became involved in the war; he was reelected again. When Truman got us into the Korean war, the American public supported him. When Eisenhower got us out, the public was even more enthusiastic.

The President is the most powerful molder of national opinion; he has access to television, radio, the press. Everything he says carries the weight of tradition and patriotism with it—even when he changes his policy, as so many presidents have done in the past. Political sociologist Seymour Lipset (in *Transaction,* September-October 1966, "The President, the Polls and Vietnam") analyzed the national poll results: "Though most Americans are willing to keep fighting in Vietnam, they clearly would prefer not to be there and are anxious and willing to turn over the responsibility to someone else. . . . The President makes opinion, he does not follow it."

The memory of the public is short; it takes little time to adjust to new realities. It accepted American toughness toward the Soviet Union. It also accepted American agreements with the Soviet Union on nuclear testing. The President has it within his power to *make* a policy politically feasible; the nation tends to rally around him, especially in foreign affairs, *whatever* his policy is. We must remember, too, that President Johnson, run-

ning on a platform of peace in Vietnam, defeated Goldwater by
an overwhelming majority when Goldwater was asking military
escalation in Vietnam. That constituency for peace still exists,
waiting for Johnson to give the word.

Of course it takes courage to change a policy, to withdraw
suddenly from a situation in which one has become more and
more involved. It takes courage to fight off the snipers, the critics,
the militarists, the fanatics. It requires either open or implied
admission of error. But this is what genuine leadership is.

President Johnson has repeatedly asked his critics: "What
do *you* suggest?" I am suggesting that the President should
appear on national television one evening, announcing before-
hand that he will make a major policy speech on Vietnam. If
he goes before the nation, announces the withdrawal of American military forces from Vietnam, and states cogently, clearly,
the reasons for this withdrawal, the American people will unite
behind him, the editorials of support will blossom everywhere,
and the angry cries of the fanatics will be drowned in an immense
and overwhelming national sigh of relief.

Many critics of our policy, who know very well that the United
States should leave Vietnam, do not want to ask immediate and
unilateral withdrawal. This is not because they find powerful
reasons against it, but because it is not a good "tactic," not "popular," not acceptable to the President and his staff.

I believe this is based on a false notion of how political decisions are made—the notion that citizens must directly persuade
the President by the soundness of their arguments. This makes
two assumptions which I think are unfounded. One is that the
interests of the citizens and the President are the same, so that
if they both think straight, they will be led to the same conclusions. Robert Michels (*Political Parties*) long ago made the classic
case for the fact that once we elect our representatives, they
develop a special interest of their own; the history of human
misery under government does much to support this. The number of Americans and Vietnamese already sent to their deaths
by decisions made in the quiet offices of President Johnson is
further evidence.

The other assumption is that the President is a rational being

who can be persuaded by rational arguments. We have seen—
and our recent foreign policy illustrates it—how our highest
officials have become the victims of myths which they themselves
help to perpetuate.

The so-called "realists" who urge us to speak softly and so
persuade the President are working against the reality, which is
that the President responds to self-interest rather than to rational
argument. Citizens can create a *new* self-interest for the President
by persuading enough of their fellow citizens, who will then
make enough of a commotion to "persuade" the President that
he had better make a change. This cannot be effectively done by
a citizenry which says only half of what it believes, which dilutes
its passion and surrenders its moral fervor. If enough people
speak for withdrawal, it can *become* politically feasible. Scholars,
newspaper editors, congressional critics fail the public when they
do not speak their full mind.

Wendell Phillips, a shrewd student of the relationship between
the politician and the citizen, once wrote: "We must ask for the
whole loaf, to get the half of it." Johnson may make a different
kind of speech; he may negotiate his way out, waiting longer,
letting more die in the interim, but getting out. He may "ar-
range" for the Saigon government to fall. (He may also drown
the world in blood, because delay and escalation invite dangerous, uncontrollable developments.)

The pressures of concerned citizens will not by themselves
change a major policy. Ultimately, a combination of factors will
probably end the war: military impasse in Vietnam, criticism
from other countries, dissatisfaction at home. Because it will be a
combination, every citizen must put his full moral weight, his
whole argument, into the balance.

When we urge Johnson to do exactly how much we *want* him
to do, and not just that little which we *expect* him to do, we are
engaging in the true politics of the citizen in a democracy, not
the sham politics of the citizen who thinks he is The Prince. Politics is not the art of the probable. It is the art of the possible. And
it is our job to insist that the politicians expand their narrow
view of what is possible.

But let us listen to the President of the United States.

10. *A Speech for LBJ*

MY FELLOW AMERICANS:

Not long ago I received a letter from my fourth-grade school teacher who still lives back in the little town where I grew up. She is of advanced age now, but still as she was when I sat in her class, a kindly and wise woman. She has been through depression and war, through sickness and the death of loved ones, more than most of us. Let me share her letter with you; I am sure she will not mind.

> Dear Lyndon: You know I have always had faith in you and knew you would do what is right. And you have been trying your best on this Vietnam situation. But nothing seems to be going right. So many people are getting killed. Not only our boys, but all those poor people over there. You have tried talking peace. And you have tried bombing, and what not. But there is no end in sight. I hear people in town saying: "We should never have gotten in, but now that we are in, we don't seem able to get out." Lyndon, can't you get us out? I am getting on now in years and would like to see peace again. God bless you.
>
> Sincerely,
Mrs. Annie Mae Lindley

Now let me read just one more letter to you. It came to me from a young man fighting with the First Marine Division in South Vietnam:

> Dear Mr. President: I am twenty years old and enlisted in the Marines as soon as I left high school in Massilon, Ohio. I have been in Vietnam six months now, and I have seen a lot. Three days ago my closest buddy was killed. Yesterday our

outfit destroyed a hamlet that Intelligence said had been used by the VC as a base. We burned the huts and threw grenades down the tunnels. But there were no VC there. In one of the tunnels there were two women and three kids. We didn't know that. One of the kids was killed and one of the women lost an eye. We rounded up all the villagers and they stood around—children, old folks, women—crying and afraid. Of course we didn't mean to kill any kids. But we did. And that's war. I know you need sometimes to do nasty things for an important cause. The trouble is—there doesn't seem much of a cause left here in Vietnam. We're supposed to be defending these people against the VC. But they don't want us to defend them. They don't care about Communism or politics or anything like that. They just want to be left in peace. So, more and more, my buddies and I wonder—what are we doing here? We're not afraid. We've been sticking it out, in the mud and in the jungle. And we'll go on like this if you ask us to. But somehow it seems wrong. I don't know what we should do, but I just thought I'd let you know how some of us feel.

> Sincerely,
> James Dixon, Corporal
> 1st Marine Division

My fellow Americans, let me tell you, I have read and reread these two letters, and they have been on my mind. You all know how my administration has been concerned with the war in Vietnam. Night after night I have sat up thinking, and sometimes—I don't mind telling you—praying, that we would find a way to end this terrible war, which has cost tens of thousands of lives, American and Vietnamese, and which has caused so much pain and suffering to millions of people in that unfortunate little country.

What have been our objectives in Vietnam? I have said many times that what we wanted was for Vietnam to be free to determine its own affairs—that this is why we were fighting. We have tried every possible way to gain this objective. We have offered negotiations. And we have fought—hard, and courageously, on unfamiliar territory—with an increasing commitment of planes, ships, and ground forces, all designed to bring the war to an end with honor.

I don't need to tell you that we have not been successful. We have not destroyed the Vietcong's will to fight. This is not a pleasant fact to report, but it is a fact.

There is another unpleasant fact to report. The government we have been supporting in Vietnam has not succeeded in gaining the respect of its own people there. No matter how valiant our men are, they cannot fight a war that is not supported by the people of the country we committed ourselves to defend. Always implied in our commitment was that if the war threatened to become *our* war, rather than a war by and for the Vietnamese, we would reconsider our position. That time has now come.

We have tried force, and we have offered negotiations. Neither has worked. Some have criticized us for not trying even more force. Of course we could do this. No one in the world needs to be told how powerful we are. We can stay in Vietnam as long as we like. We can reduce the whole country to ashes. We are powerful enough to do this. But we are not cruel enough to do this. I, as your President, am not willing to engage in a war without end that would destroy the youth of this nation and the people of Vietnam.

We had hoped this war could end by negotiations. But this has not worked. Pride and self-respect have often stood in the way for both sides. We are not willing to beg for negotiations. And we have too much compassion for those dying each day in Vietnam to let the war continue. In Korea, you may remember, the war dragged on, while the negotiators tried to agree on terms. The diplomats talked, while men died. For two years they talked, and for two years the corpses piled up in that unfortunate land. We do not want that kind of negotiation in Vietnam.

The American people have the courage to fight. We have shown this a dozen times in the past, from Bunker Hill to Gettysburg, from Normandy to Guadalcanal. We also have the courage to *stop* fighting, not when someone else decides for us, but when *we* decide for ourselves.

As Commander-in-Chief of the armed forces, I have ordered

that, as of midnight tonight, our Air Force and our Navy will halt the bombings in North and South Vietnam. We have not run out of planes, nor have we run out of bombs, nor have we run out of the determination to use them when it is wise. What we *have* run out of is the willingness to see more people die under our bombs. Too many have died. Too many have suffered. It is time to call a halt.

Also, I have given orders to General Westmoreland, the capable and courageous Commander of our forces in Vietnam, to halt offensive operations and to begin the orderly withdrawal of our armed forces from that country.

Let us speak frankly now about the consequences of this decision.

We may see a period of turmoil and conflict in Vietnam. But that was true before we arrived. That is the nature of the world. It is hard to imagine, however, any conflict that will be more destructive than what is going on now. Our departure will inevitably diminish the fighting. It may end it.

There are many places in the world where people are going through the disorder and the violence of social change. The United States cannot interfere in every one of those instances. We do not intend to do so. To the extent that the United Nations can mediate in helping to bring tranquility to Vietnam, we will happily lend our moral and financial support.

Vietnam may become a Communist nation. The northern half of that country has been Communist for some time, and a good part of the population in the South has been sympathetic to the Vietcong. Desperate people often turn to Communism. But we have shown that we can live in peace with Communist nations, if there is mutual respect. Despite our many disagreements, we have maintained peaceful relations with the Soviet Union, with Yugoslavia, with Poland, with other Communist nations. We can certainly live in peace with Vietnam.

Everyone knows that behind our military activity in Vietnam has been our concern that Communist China shall not press its weight on other countries. Many experts on China have told us that much of China's belligerent attitude has been due to nationalistic feeling and to her fear that we intend to attack her. I hereby give my pledge that the United States will never initiate a war with China, and we will begin soon to seek ways and means of coming to a more amicable relationship with her.

I have often said that the most effective means of maintaining a free society does not consist of armed might, but of economic development and prosperity. That will be our aim now in Asia. Our military bases will now be able to give way to dams, to factories, to hydroelectric plants. From now on, our war will be on starvation and disease, on misery and hopelessness. Our skills and our resources will be used, no longer to destroy, but to build —to build a new life for the children now growing up in Asia.

To this end, I am going to ask Congress to take half of the $20 billion allocated for the Vietnam war this year and to put it into a fund—an international fund, if the United Nations will set this up—for the economic development of Vietnam and other countries in Southeast Asia. We will not force our favors upon these countries. But we will stand ready to help—with no political strings attached—on the basis of their own declarations, their own needs.

The war in Vietnam was beginning to slow down many of our plans for the Great Society—plans to end poverty, to build homes and schools, to rebuild our cities, to eliminate the slums which have been at the root of unrest in various parts of the country. There will be $10 billion left unused from the war. I will ask Congress to redirect that money for purposes which I will outline in a special message next week.

We have made an important decision. It is a decision based on a fundamental American belief that human life is sacred, that peace is precious, and that true power does not consist in the brute force of guns and bombs, but in the economic well-being of a free people.

The dream I have always had since I was a boy in Texas, I still have—and I want to fulfill it for America. We are about to embark on a venture far more glorious, far more bold, requiring far more courage—than war. Our aim is to build a society which will set an example for the rest of mankind. I am happy to stand before you tonight and to say that we will now build this Great Society in earnest.

I need not tell you how long I have waited for this moment—and how happy I am to be able to say that now, after so much pain, after so much sacrifice, our boys will be coming home.

My fellow Americans, good night and sleep well. We are no longer at war in Vietnam.

Index

Books by Howard Zinn available from Haymarket Books

Disobedience and Democracy
Nine Fallacies on Law and Order

ᴥ

Failure to Quit
Reflections of an Optimistic Historian

ᴥ

Vietnam
The Logic of Withdrawal

ᴥ

SNCC
The New Abolitionists

ᴥ

The Southern Mystique

ᴥ

Justice in Everyday Life
The Way It Really Works

ᴥ

Postwar America
1945–1971

ᴥ

Emma
A Play in Two Acts About Emma Goldman, American Anarchist

ᴥ

Marx in Soho
A Play on History

order online from HaymarketBooks.org